Tree of Life Coaching

Practical Secrets of the Kabbalah for Coaches and Hypnosis and NLP Practitioners

By

Shawn Carson

Changing Mind Publishing
New York, New York

Tree of Life Coaching: Practical Kabbalah for Coaches and Hypnosis and NLP Practitioners

Photography courtesy of Caroline Bergonzi

Table of Contents

Illustrations

Foreword
By Mark Simmons

When I met Shawn Carson he was teaching the Meta Pattern and as a "Jungian" and student of Kabbalah I immediately was captivated by the lining up of opposites, the association of the problem in earthly, sensation grounded experience, followed by a solicitation of resource and then, a collapsed integration between the newly anchored resource and the real-life contextual experience. To me this was Jacob's Ladder, The Tree of Life, brought to awareness and joined elegantly, bringing the new and unconscious into the here and now and into matter as is its higher intent. And that tipping point of new reality requires a future pacing of integrated experience in several other earthly contexts in order to induct into a true new reality.

Shawn also taught and utilized the Jigsaw Pattern which reminds me of a checklist of logical levels , contextual possibilities and attributes that determine what's happening now. And in the Jigsaw Pattern I saw the Tree of Life and became hopeful that one day I could use the more complete Tree of Life to work on myself and coach others. I knew the key was to be able to access and utilize the Tree of Life experientially. This is important because I believe that the Tree of Life offers the most complete model for change and transformation in personal, group and world and that this requires a visceral, conscious and active participation in the Tree of Life's patterns, structure, energy and meaning.

I gave Shawn a book, Tarot and the Tree of Life by Isabel Kliegman,"
a book on the Minor Arcana of Tarot that uses the Tree of Life as the
main system and metaphor to explain the worldly, contextual situation
of each card. Within each card lies the Map of the World at play, the
thoughts, beliefs, values, energies, rites of passage, personality types,
archetypes, identity and life task contained within the card. The cards
have movement and symbolic connection to each of the sephirot, their
implied purpose and meaning in the cycle of life. Trusting his own
experience Shawn noticed how the historic Tree of Life was set up as
a Mirror image of himself, how the map of the ten sephirot
encompassing four worlds maps the universe as we know it. Adding to
many experiences from Hypnosois and NLP Shawn became aware of
the personal growth and coaching possibilities within the 22 paths on
the Tree. From NLP Shawn recognized that the essence characteristics
and positions of the Ten Sephirot were identical with NLP eye
accessing positions and body experiences, which he knew and trusted
from working on himself and hundreds of clients. Shawn said that he
reversed the right and the left of the historical Tree so that the Tree of
Life would be in the position of the client. Reflecting a new generation
of individuals and practitioners who value their own experience,
Shawn saw the need to experience the Tree from within and not from
the outside or top down. Most conventional Tree of Life learning is
Top-Down. In the dream of Jacob's Ladder the Angels are going up
and down the ladder. Today this revelation is still ignored. As the
angels go up and down a loop forms and completes the circuit system
between heaven and earth. The loop includes the returning light that
manifests the new reality and creates every experience, belief and
material revelation you know. Shawn knew that change requires
experience and participation in the whole loop not just the context
point of one problem.

Each of the ten sephirot is an entry point and an essence
characteristic, each a field, and earth unto itself. Ten stations on the
tree of life, where experience can be changed, attention can be altered,
rescurce can be noticed and personal history can be transformed. As
paths are traveled new loops completed, the Tree provides context,
pattern and framework for the most transformational work making

material changes take place, creating new neuro-pathways and changing history.

Kircher's Tree of Life

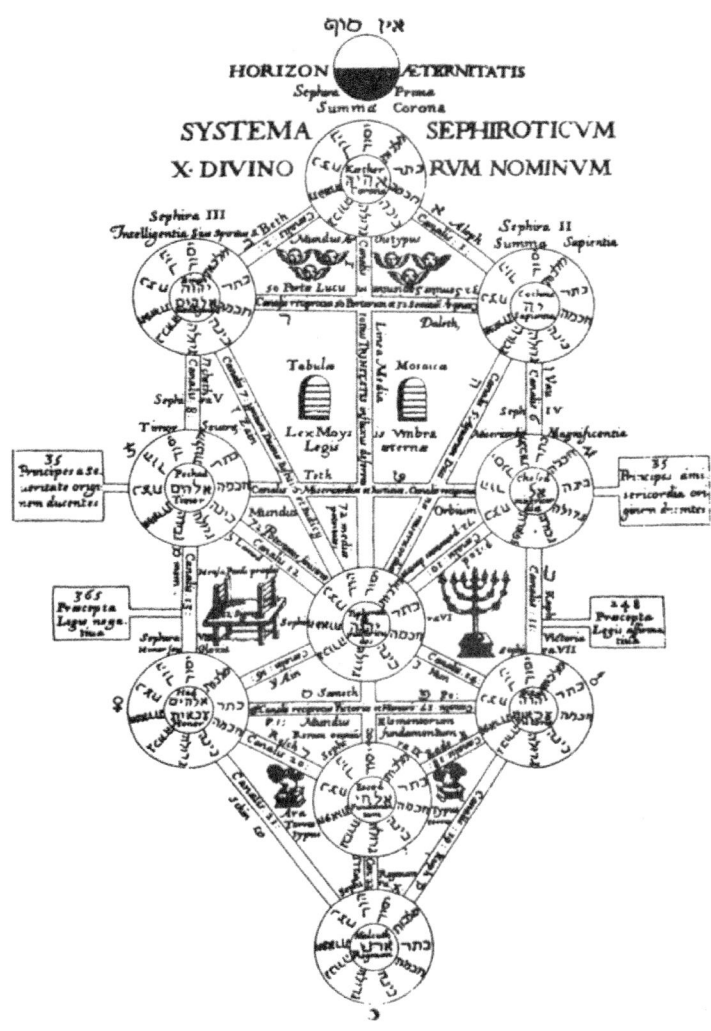

Self Coaching Tree of Life
(Your Tree)

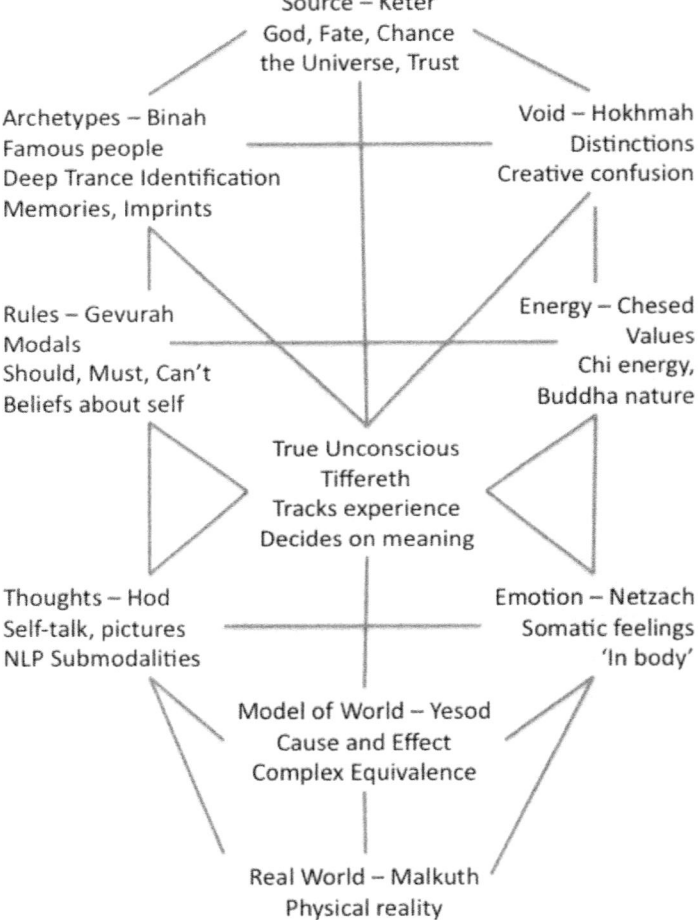

Source – Keter
God, Fate, Chance
the Universe, Trust

Archetypes – Binah
Famous people
Deep Trance Identification
Memories, Imprints

Void – Hokhmah
Distinctions
Creative confusion

Rules – Gevurah
Modals
Should, Must, Can't
Beliefs about self

Energy – Chesed
Values
Chi energy,
Buddha nature

True Unconscious
Tiffereth
Tracks experience
Decides on meaning

Thoughts – Hod
Self-talk, pictures
NLP Submodalities

Emotion – Netzach
Somatic feelings
'In body'

Model of World – Yesod
Cause and Effect
Complex Equivalence

Real World – Malkuth
Physical reality

Coaching Tree of Life
(Your Client's Tree)

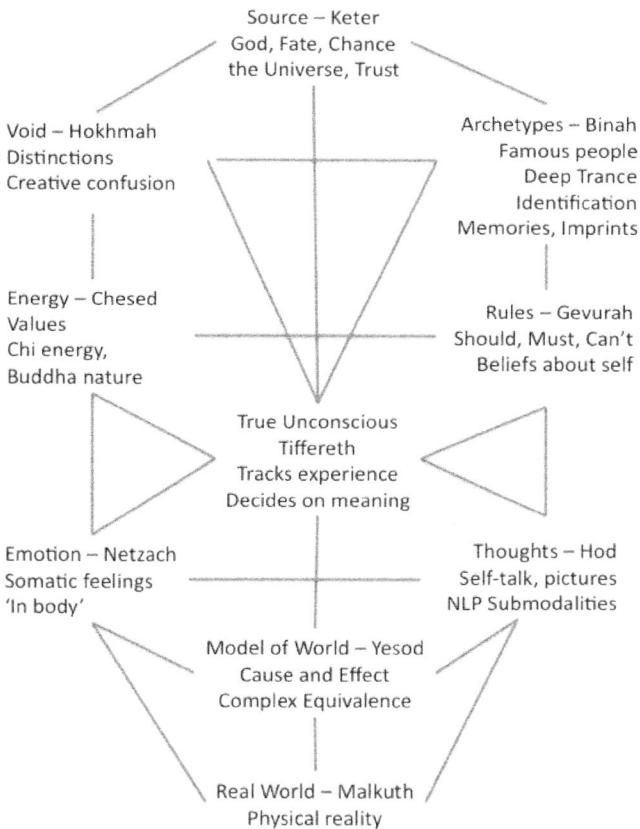

Source – Keter
God, Fate, Chance
the Universe, Trust

Void – Hokhmah
Distinctions
Creative confusion

Archetypes – Binah
Famous people
Deep Trance
Identification
Memories, Imprints

Energy – Chesed
Values
Chi energy,
Buddha nature

Rules – Gevurah
Should, Must, Can't
Beliefs about self

True Unconscious
Tiffereth
Tracks experience
Decides on meaning

Emotion – Netzach
Somatic feelings
'In body'

Thoughts – Hod
Self-talk, pictures
NLP Submodalities

Model of World – Yesod
Cause and Effect
Complex Equivalence

Real World – Malkuth
Physical reality

Introduction to the Tree of Life

Mark Simmons turned to me and, out of the blue, told me:

"You should study the Tree of Life!"

Because I know Mark very well, I'm quite used to his apparent non sequiturs, and I've learned that they often contain hidden wisdom. I was familiar with the Tree of Life from conversations with many of my NLP students who had also studied Kabbalah, but had never felt drawn to it.

"Mark, my impression is that Kabbalah is purposefully complex in order to guard its secrets. I'm not sure I have the time nor the inclination to study it."

"Read *Tarot and the Tree of Life* by Isabel Kliegman. She lays it out in a simple way that even you'll be able to understand!" Mark grinned.

Now, the truth of the matter is that most of the books that people tell me to read are really not very interesting to me. But sometimes they are very interesting. So when someone recommends a book to me, I'm likely to read it on the chance that it could transform my life. So I followed Mark's advice and read something that did transform my life.

Ms. Kliegman's book explains the correspondence between the Tarot and the Tree of Life. It's a relatively short book, just over two hundred pages. The second chapter of the book, at about twenty-five pages, discusses the Tree of Life and the branches of the Tree of Life (which are called Sephirot in Kabbalah, but I will refer to them as branches).

As Ms. Kliegman described each branch, moving down the Tree of Life, I suddenly realized that there is a one-to-one correspondence between the branches of the Tree of Life and the eye-accessing cues of NLP. And I became really excited. I'll explain why in a moment, but before I do, I'd better explain NLP eye accessing.

NLP has a theory that as you think about things, or remember things, the movement of your eyes—up or down, to the left or to the right— offers very specific clues about *how* you are thinking. There's actually a lot of scientific research about eye movement and cognitive processes (which my colleagues and I plan to discuss in a future book, titled *Eye Accessing*, in our NLP Mastery series). But NLP eye accessing did not arise from the Tree of Life or the Kabbalah—it arose from early NLP practitioners observing their clients.

So why did I get so excited by this random association between the Tree of Life and NLP? The reason I got so excited is because when you see that the structure of two apparently unrelated things is the same, you know you have discovered a deeper truth that underlies both of them. It's this "truth" that this book seeks to explain.

Before I talk about this in more depth, I need to take you back in time, when I was first exposed to the ideas of coaching through the study of NLP. I was first introduced to coaching as a client. I was working for a large global consulting firm and was offered some coaching sessions to improve my personal effectiveness. This was back in 1993. Unfortunately, I don't remember the name of my coach, but she had the most profound effect on me. One of the things she did was to introduce me to the book *Influencing with Integrity* by Genie Z. Laborde, which still has an honored place in my library. Prior to reading Dr. Laborde's book, people had been something of a mystery to me. I knew that everyone was different, that everyone had his or her own personality. But I had no way of talking about, or even thinking about, how any particular person "worked," other than by using bland generalizations. I might consider one person to be a "leader" and another a "team player," but I didn't have any framework for really understanding how or why people did what they did.

Dr. Laborde's book introduced me to the basic concepts of NLP. One definition of NLP is "the study of subjective experience." NLP provides a set of concepts, and a vocabulary, to describe very fine distinctions about different individuals—how and why one person differs from another. I was captivated by NLP. I read a number of books on NLP in the decade that followed, but I wasn't able to begin to really master NLP until I semiretired from corporate consulting in 2006.

In 2006, I was in the middle of a very successful, time-consuming, and stressful career as a consultant, advising multinational corporations on how to structure their operations. This provided the perfect mix of sufficient money and sufficient dissatisfaction to persuade me to resign and begin to study NLP, hypnosis, coaching, and other related disciplines on a full-time basis. I became a certified hypnotist, coach, NLP Master Practitioner, and NLP and hypnosis trainer, and I absorbed a huge body of information.

However, I had no unifying system that tied it all together. Then I discovered the Tree of Life through Ms. Kliegman. I dived into a deep study of the Tree of Life in order to uncover this deeper truth—a truth that could be glimpsed in disciplines as diverse as the Kabbalah and NLP and, of course, the Tarot. As I did so, I discovered the structure underlying every form of coaching I have ever seen, including NLP, hypnosis, Jungian therapy, and also ancient systems such as tai chi. This is the structure I will be showing you in this book.

In fact, the more I learned, the more I became certain that the Tree of Life provides a complete description of the human experience. It doesn't just offer a structure for coaching, but for *any* human interaction, whether in personal relationships, business, or sports. It even seems to apply to warfare, and in fact, one of my big aha moments came when I was reading the work of the fighter pilot and military theorist John Boyd and realized that this theory of the "OODA Loop" was the fighter pilot's description of the Tree of Life!

In this book, I am going to describe the structure of the Tree of Life. I am going to explain how that structure underlies human experience. And I am going to explain how you can use the Tree of Life in your coaching work, no matter what type of coaching you do.

I'm going to explain how every meaningful experience has to be rooted in a specific context, real time, and place. Without rooting experience in reality, it ultimately means nothing.

I'm going to explain how the world we believe we inhabit doesn't correspond to reality. Reality is a complex exchange of matter and energy existing in a web of time and space. The all too limited human brain is not able to fully comprehend or process reality. Instead, your brain uses a brilliant set of heuristics and estimates, which I refer to as your individual Sensory Model of the World. Your Sensory Model of the World contains models of cause-and-effect relationships that allow you to predict what will happen in the Real World when you take a specific action (although, of course, these predictions are not always correct!).

I'm going to explain how your thoughts create representations of the predictions generated by your Sensory Model of the World and how your emotions provide you with the emotional energy to act on these predictions.

I'm going to explain how your brain uses experience to write a rule book for you in order to simplify your decision making. And I am going to explain how your body generates its own rules based on enduring feelings, or states of being, to guide your actions.

I'm going to explain how your memories—memories of your own actions as well as the actions of other people you have known, seen, or read about—provide you with a database of archetypal responses to all sorts of potential situations.

And I'm going to explain what your mind does when it can't find the answer. When the answer can't be predicted by your Sensory Model of the World and isn't in your rule book, nor in your database of archetypal responses, your mind is set up to generate a unique creative response to the situation.

And I'm going to explain how your amazing unconscious mind tracks the sensory information you receive from the world around you, your physical emotions, and your mental thoughts—how it makes sense of all this using your internal rule book and database of archetypal responses, how it generates unique creative solutions when necessary, and how it turns all of this into behaviors.

Finally, I'm going to explain how the random hand of chance, of fate, perhaps even the hand of God, changes everything. And I'm going to explain how all these things fit together in one unifying structure that I refer to as the Tree of Life.

But I only have the time and space to scratch the surface of the Tree of Life. There are so many facets to this fascinating tool, this description of human experience, that its applications are virtually unlimited. If you spend time experiencing your own Tree of Life, you will find applications that I have never even considered. I wish you good luck in your journey!

Shawn Carson
New York
2015

Chapter 1: The Tree of Life, Jacob's Ladder, and the Kabbalah

A long time ago, there was a wise man who was on a long journey through an ancient desert. One day as the sun set, this man stopped to rest. With nothing but a stone as his pillow, he drifted off to sleep. This was no ordinary sleep because on this night, the wise man was shown the pathway to God.

The wise man dreamed of a ladder to Heaven. On this ladder, angels were both ascending and descending. The ladder itself only had four steps, and although small in number, these steps contained the whole of existence. The first rung of the ladder, the one closest to Earth, was the world of action. This was the physical world—the place where the laws of nature and science apply. The second step was the world of formation. This is where reality is constructed through an understanding of the Real World, Thought, Emotion, Rules, and Energy. This step is the formation of subjective reality. The next step up the ladder was the world of creation. This is the world of Archetypes and, even beyond that, Wisdom or emptiness from which there is infinite potential for creation to spring. The highest step, the rung that is in Heaven, is the world of intimacy. This is the meeting point between the soul and God.

Just as the angels moved up and down the ladder, so too do humans move up the ladder, and God's energy moves down. When the wise man awoke, he knew that this ladder is the direct link between God and humans.

This is a book about coaching, a method of coaching that's built around a model for living life—your life and your client's life. The model is described using the metaphor of a tree, and in fact the model is called the Tree of Life. You may well be asking, "Why another coaching model? Aren't there enough coaching models out there already?" That's a great question and one that I will begin to answer in this chapter.

Suppose I told you that there is a coaching model that has stood the test of time. How long might you think that model has been around? Ten years? Twenty years? Fifty years? In fact, the model has been around for at least seven hundred years (as I will be demonstrating), and it may well have been around for much longer. Some people argue that the model describes how the universe itself was created.

Now, I am not going to argue that this model is "true" or that reality actually corresponds to this model. Reality is what it is, and any model of reality is just that—a model. Having said this, in order to function in the Real World, to understand other people as well as yourself, and to achieve your dreams, you have to have a useful description or model—one that allows you to navigate reality. This means that you have to distinguish one thing from another, to call one thing a "belief" and another thing a "value," to distinguish "thoughts" from "emotions" and "conscious thought" from the "unconscious mind." Now, these things are not "true," and you can argue that none of them actually exist in reality, that they are just concepts. But they are useful, and that's what counts.

So the Tree of Life is seven hundred years old and is a useful model of reality. In the beginning, the Tree of Life model was vague, even cryptic. The first mention of the Tree of Life occurs in the Bible, which says that two trees stood in the Garden of Eden—the Tree of Knowledge and the Tree of Life. It appears a number of times in the Torah, although in a more cryptic manner. More explicit details of the

Tree of Life were revealed in the Middle Ages in the famous Kabbalistic book the Zohar. The Tree of Life was updated "recently" into its modern form, but even this "recent" update took place almost four hundred years ago! Therefore, if longevity is any indication of the quality of a model, the Tree of Life is the best coaching model there is.

Personally, I value the Tree of Life because I believe it offers the most complete, and yet simplest, description of the human experience that exists. If you follow the teachings of the Tree of Life, you will find that you have control over your own emotions and thoughts, and that you'll be able to discover a model of reality that will serve you well through any situation or experience you may have.

But perhaps you're not interested in how long a model has been in existence or its practical applications. Perhaps you're more of a spiritual person and you're more interested in how deeply the model can connect you to your true spiritual self, to the spiritual energy of the universe, perhaps even to God. If you are interested in deepening your spiritual connection to the universe, it's good to know that the Tree of Life model comes from the spiritual discipline of Jewish Kabbalah and that the Tree of Life is a symbol that is mentioned in the Christian Old Testament. The Tree of Life was used as a tool of meditation by arguably the most spiritual of the Christian orders—the Jesuits. The Tree of Life Model has also been adopted by a number of New Age disciplines, from tarot and astrology to acupuncture and the study of the chakras. If you want a coaching system that is deeply rooted in mysticism and spirituality, the Tree of Life is it.

Perhaps you are more practical. Maybe you don't care how long a system has been around or whether it contains a lot of "woo-woo" concepts—you simply want something that works across as many different situations as possible. My colleagues and I are professional hypnotists and coaches. We see all sorts of clients with all sorts of issues, and we teach all sorts of courses to all sorts of audiences. I have helped people quit smoking, I have coached professional athletes and high-level business leaders. I have taught coaching skills to business managers, business coaches, hypnotists, social workers, and psychiatrists. And in all the time I've been coaching, I've never coached a person whose issues could not be described, accurately and completely, and changed effectively, using the Tree of Life model. Nor have I ever seen a hypnosis, NLP, or coaching pattern that could not be described using the Tree of Life model. It is not necessary to understand the Tree of Life to be a great coach or hypnotist; however, when you do understand the Tree of Life, you will be able to break down what any great coach or hypnotist is doing. You'll be able to find the perfect technique to help any client.

So, whether you're seeking to discover your true values, let go of limiting beliefs, find joy in your life, take control of your thoughts, or simply achieve more success in the world, the Tree of Life will help you, and your clients, do that.

History of the Tree of Life

In the rest of this chapter, I am going to very briefly touch on some of the history of the Tree of Life model, from the Torah and Old Testament to the primary text of Jewish Kabbalah, the Zohar, to the Jesuit text *Oedipus Aegyptiacus*, written by Athanasius Kircher in 1652, which illustrates the Tree of Life in its modern form. Now personally, I find it interesting to know the background of things and where they came from. It makes me feel more connected to them. However, if you're the sort of person who doesn't care where something came from, only how it's used, you won't lose anything by skipping the rest of this chapter.

The Tree of Life is mentioned in the book of Genesis in the Old Testament. It is said that there were two trees growing at the center of the Garden of Eden—the Tree of Life and the Tree of Knowledge. The Tree of Knowledge caused all sorts of problems for Adam and Eve, eventually leading them to be expelled from the Garden of Eden. Little is said about the Tree of Life, but it's good to know that we can safely eat its fruit!

18

There is another biblical story I should mention that is often associated with the Tree of Life, and that is the story of Jacob. Jacob was traveling and, at nightfall, set up camp using a stone as a pillow. During the night, he dreamed, and somehow he knew that this dream was important. He dreamed that he saw a staircase reaching from Earth to Heaven, with angels ascending and descending the staircase. There are many interpretations of this story, but one belief is that the staircase Jacob saw represents the Tree of Life. In this interpretation, the image of angels ascending and descending represents the idea that if you wish, you can become your true authentic self by using the Tree of Life to ascend through the levels of your own being. You can even ascend through the divine creative act as far as heaven itself and even see God. This idea of using the Tree of Life to ascend back to the divine is taken up by the Kabbalah in the book the Zohar.

The Tree of Life as a detailed metaphor dates back to the early days of the Kabbalah, a form of Jewish mysticism that became formalized in the Zohar. The Zohar was published in the thirteenth century by Moses de Leon. The Zohar is written in a quite difficult, even confusing, way. You see, it was believed that the secrets of the Zohar should only be revealed to those who were willing to study its secrets—secrets that could lead to union with the divine. But don't worry; our intention in this book is to make things as easy as possible!

I say the Zohar was "published" because the Zohar was purportedly written by a Jewish rabbi named Rashbi who lived in the second century CE, and even then it was based upon much earlier teachings. In fact, some adherents of Kabbalah trace its origins back to the Garden of Eden, through the book of Genesis, as noted above. While the true origins of the Tree of Life as a metaphor are uncertain, we do know that it was around in at least the thirteenth century, i.e., at least seven hundred years ago.

The Zohar suggests that the Tree of Life is a metaphor for creation on several levels. It's a metaphor for the creation of the universe from the Big Bang, to the creation of individual atoms out of the energy created by the Big Bang, to the creation of our galaxy, our sun, our solar system, and our own Planet Earth. It's a metaphor for the creation of life, including humans. It's also a metaphor for the development of human civilization and, within a civilization, of each individual human experience.

However, the Tree of Life is much more than just a metaphor. The Tree of Life offers a practical tool for an individual to reascend to the Source of creation (you can think of this Source as being God if you believe in God, or simply the underlying reality on which the universe is based). Having reached the Source and experienced "divine inspiration," the Tree of Life allows you to return to the Real World, bringing this knowledge with you.

I hope to offer you some clues as to how to do this, and how you can help your clients find their own spiritual self, in the pages of this book!

The Tree of Life went through various forms before becoming more or less fixed in the way it is most commonly seen today and the way that I will be describing it in this book. Athanasius Kircher, a Jesuit priest and polymath who studied fields as diverse as Egyptian hieroglyphics, mathematics, geology, medicine, and theology, and who is often compared to Leonardo da Vinci, illustrated this "modern" interpretation of the Tree of Life. Kircher included an illustration of the Tree of Life in his book *Oedipus Aegyptiacus*, which was written in 1652. Prior to Kircher, the actual structure of the Tree of Life was unclear because it was described in words rather than in pictures. Once Kircher provided his illustration, that became the way the Tree of Life has always been drawn, up to and including modern times.

I will be using Kircher's Tree of Life as my metaphor in this book, so it is worthwhile to take a look at the diagram at the beginning on page 7.

In the next chapter, I will provide a quick tour—, an overview—of Tree of Life Coaching.

Chapter 2: What is Tree of Life Coaching

We all have problems. I have problems, you have problems, everyone has problems. As a coach, your job is to help your clients work through their problems and find solutions. Of course, different coaches use different approaches, depending upon their training and experience. After all, there are many coaching systems available.

So how is Tree of Life Coaching different? Well, you can think of Tree of Life Coaching in several different ways. It is:

- A tool kit to add to your coaching toolbox. Tree of Life Coaching contains many powerful techniques to help your clients.
- A tool to help you, as a coach, to understand any coaching system and to select the coaching system that suits you best, or to combine techniques from different modalities to create your own coaching system
- A complete system of coaching in and of itself

When you work with a client, a great place to start the process is to listen to, and understand, exactly what it is that your client wants to achieve and what it is that is stopping him. (For this example, I will be using the pronoun *he* throughout.) Your client will have an outcome—something he wants in his life. And he will have a problem, something that is preventing him from having his outcome right now. A smoker's outcome is to be smoke-free, and the cigarettes, or rather his habit of smoking cigarettes, is the problem that prevents him from being smoke-free. A coaching client might have as the outcome to earn $1 million a year (his outcome), but he might not feel as focused on the tasks he has to complete to reach this outcome, and this lack of focus is his problem.

Sometimes a client's problem arises from real events in the Real World. These types of problems may not be amenable to being solved through coaching (although the client's feelings *about* the problem may be). For example, perhaps I forget to buy milk on my way home, or I lose a loved one, or my house burns down because I left the gas on. These are Real World problems and have Real World solutions: I drink my coffee black for the night; I grieve and move on; I call my insurance company to file a claim and then buy a new house.

But other types of problems arise because of a client's internal world. For example, perhaps I help my neighbor paint his house, but when I ask him to help me repair my fence, he refuses, leaving me hurt and confused. As a result, I have unwanted thoughts and feelings that seem to spiral around inside me, leaving me no energy to focus on anything else. My problem is not that I can't fix my own fence (or if that is the problem, I can simply pay a contractor to do it); rather, it's how I *feel* about what happened.

Perhaps your client has beliefs about himself that limit his ability to live his dreams. He thinks he'll never have the career that he wants, and he stops trying. His problem is not his lack of a career; it's his lack of motivation that arises out of his limiting belief.

Or perhaps he pursues dreams of fame and riches, when he would be better off pursuing happiness. He spends his entire life in the office, working hard to gain promotions, earning pay rises and bonuses that he either doesn't have the time to spend or spends on things he doesn't need and doesn't really want. He might feel successful but unfulfilled, and it is his lack of a feeling of fulfillment that is his problem.

It could be that he unconsciously models himself on a parent whose own life was disastrous and begins to follow the same path that the parent did. Perhaps his father was an alcoholic, and he becomes one as well. Or perhaps he uses his parents' disastrous marriage as the model for his own.

Or perhaps he has lost sight of the unlimited potential of the universe. He becomes caught in a dead-end career or a loveless marriage and simply can't create any alternatives for himself.

He may even have lost touch with God herself. He may forget to ask, "Why am I here?" with a sense of awe and wonder.

These types of internal problems require us to reassess our lives in some way—from the inside out, as it were. Perhaps we need to view the world in a different way, or think different thoughts, or feel different feelings. Perhaps we need to modify what we believe about ourselves and our place in the world. Or we need to reassess the relative values of those things that we hold most dear. Perhaps we need to take on a new role model. Or we may even need to open ourselves up to the possibilities of the universe, or even to the Source of universal energy (whatever you perceive that to be).

To do this, you need some kind of guide. This may be a spiritual or religious guide, a role model, a guru, a mentor, a friend, a teacher, or just someone in whom you confide. In addition to a person, it may be a book, a system, or some other way of learning. On a more practical level, some people will look to a coach. What is certain is that we can't solve a problem using the same level of logic that we used to create it (to paraphrase Albert Einstein). We need to step outside of our current reality long enough to find a new reality. And that's exactly what Tree of Life Coaching is about.

There are many different types of coaching. A coach, or coaching system, may show you some method for succeeding in the world. Some coaches will tell you what to do, and what to say, and who to meet to make your fortune. Others may tell you how to use the power of your thoughts to create the life you want using visualization, mental rehearsal, positive affirmations, or some other way of controlling your thoughts. Some coaching systems will show you how to feel confident or happy, no matter what. Still other systems will spin stories that will change what you believe about the possibilities that are open to you— perhaps stories of people who overcame great hardship to achieve success (*and so can you!*). Some may use values-based coaching that leverages what is really important in your life, what you really want, to change your behaviors for the better, and others will show you how to live in harmony with the energy of your own body through physical arts such as yoga or tai chi. Some systems will suggest that you study the great men and women who have come before so as to better make your own mark on the world. And some will lead you to deep states of meditation and even show you how to access the divine.

Tree of Life Coaching is a coaching system that incorporates all of the above. This may sound like a grandiose claim, but as you will soon see, this is actually the very basis of Tree of Life Coaching. The system that I will show you will allow you to change your thoughts, your feelings, your beliefs, and your values, and will allow you to tap into the minds of the geniuses of history and the unity of the universe. And it does so in a way that is simple to understand.

This is indeed a grandiose claim, and, as I explained in Chapter 1, I make it only because the system has been around for a thousand years, linking behavior in the everyday world with the divine and everything in between.

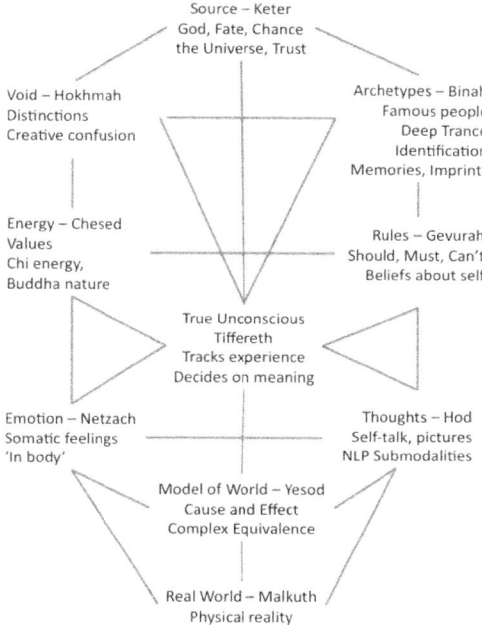

Definition of Tree of Life Coaching

I will use the following definition of Tree of Life Coaching for the purposes of this book:

Tree of Life Coaching is a system that is based on the Tree of Life from the Kabbalah. The client's Tree of Life is explored, with the help of the coach, to discover the structure of the client's problem within his or her Tree of Life. The client's Tree of Life is then rebalanced, or perhaps I should say regrown, using one or more coaching tools. As a result of this rebalancing, the problem is eliminated, and a new, resourceful client emerges with a new, healthier Tree of Life.

As its name suggests, Tree of Life Coaching can be thought of as an organic process. Using Tree of Life Coaching, you as a coach can carefully prune the client's Tree to replace any unhealthy branches, or

25

you can remove the client's problem Tree entirely, allowing a new Tree to grow in its place. We can never be sure exactly how this new Tree will grow, so the coach must become a gardener—a human arborist—guiding the client's Tree to grow in a healthy way.

The Tree of Life as a Coaching Tool

The Tree of Life model allows you to completely map out your client's outcome and the problem that is currently preventing him or her from reaching his or her outcome. This will allow you to identify the specific areas of your client's life—his or her thoughts and emotional states, beliefs, values, and the identity-level issues where he or she must make changes in order to achieve his or her outcome.

As I describe the branches and structure of the Tree of Life in the chapters that follow, I will provide you with a number of different coaching tools that can be used to generate change in each of these branches. Feel free to add these tools to your coaching tool kit and to use these patterns whenever you come across a client who is struggling in that particular branch of his or her Tree of Life. Even changing one branch may generate an entirely new and improved Tree of Life for a client. Knowing that you have tools to change any branch that needs to be pruned is an enormous confidence boost!

The Tree of Life as a Coaching Framework

There are very many coaching tools and techniques that can be incorporated into, and understood in the context of, Tree of Life Coaching. Indeed, as I will show, each and every coaching modality that currently exists focuses on changing one or more branches in a client's Tree of Life. Therefore, any coaching modality you currently use can be incorporated into Tree of Life Coaching.

If nothing else, understanding the principles of the Tree of Life will allow you to better understand the coaching or change modality that you use. The Tree of Life can act as a conceptual framework to help you understand your own coaching style.

26

The Tree of Life as a Complete Coaching System

The Tree of Life can also be thought of as a complete coaching system. The Tree of Life Coaching system will provide you with:

- A complete vocabulary that will allow you to fully understand the coaching process
- Tools to "diagnose" (note that I am using the word *diagnose* in an everyday English language meaning; you should not try to medically diagnose anyone unless you are medically qualified) exactly where your client has to make changes in his or her life, including a complete map of where the client is now as well as where he or she wants to get to
- Tools to make very specific changes in each aspect of your client's experience in order to allow your client to reach his or her outcomes
- Tools to generalize and spread these changes throughout the entirety of your client's life experience, i.e., throughout his or her Tree of Life

In this book, I will be showing you how to coach through various areas of the Tree of Life. I will also be showing you a traditional technique from the Kabbalah called the lightning path. The lightning path is a traditional way to first ascend, and then descend, the Tree of Life, visiting every branch along the way. During the ascent, you will have the opportunity to identify any part of your Tree (or your client's Tree) that is not in line with who you want to be. In short, any point in the Tree that is part of some problem in your life can be visited, pruned, and, if necessary, replaced.

Having ascended the Tree of Life to the top, you will have access to the source of all energy in the universe, which allows you to utterly transform yourself and your life. You will then have the opportunity to descend, bringing that energy with you, transforming and revitalizing all the branches of the Tree. I'll talk about this technique in detail in Chapter 7.

For now, let's take a moment to briefly explore the individual branches of the Tree of Life within the specific context of coaching. I will start from the bottom of the Tree and work my way up. For now, I am only going to describe the coaching interpretation of each branch. I will give a little more information on the meaning of the branch within the Kabbalah in Chapters 16-25, which discusses each specific branch.

In this book, I am going to give you the name that I use in Tree of Life Coaching as well as the traditional Hebrew name for each of the branches (together with the common English translation of the Hebrew name). This will allow you to do further research on each of the branches if you wish to. Please note that you will find different spellings of the Hebrew names in different books and online resources, and you may also find slight variances in the English translations. The format will be:

Tree of Life Coaching name – Hebrew name – English translation of the Hebrew

For the purposes of this review, we will consider a specific example: supposing you have a coaching client who comes to you for help with presentation skills and public speaking.

The Lower Triad

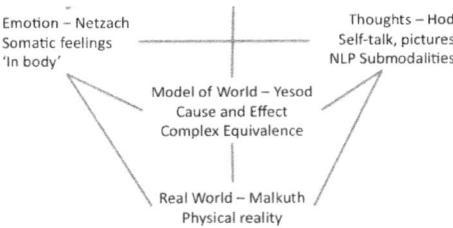

The Real World – Malkuth – The Kingdom

Some people need help with presentation skills because they literally don't know what to do. Unfortunately for those of us who attend a lot of trainings, especially corporate trainings, some of these people are correct—they *don't* know what to do! For example, some presenters believe that the best way to teach is to type out the entire presentation on PowerPoint slides and then read the slides to you with the lights turned out (so you can better read the slides to yourself). This is indeed a wonderful way to take a short nap after lunch on an all-day course, but not so effective if you actually want people to learn.

So the first step in helping your client, if he or she presents this way, might be to teach him or her good, Real World presentation skills!

Another type of Real World problem that can arise is when the speaker doesn't understand how to use his or her own body and the importance of doing so purposefully. For some who have anxiety about speaking in public, this may result in a distracting sort of "dance" where they shift their weight from one foot to the other, almost as if their unconscious mind is try to get them to walk off the stage! I remember watching one quite polished speaker give a presentation, but for the whole time she was speaking, her right foot would slowly leave the ground and her right leg would bend up behind her, almost as if she were a flamingo. The foot would then slowly descend and return to the ground. This strange dance continued during her entire presentation.

Once you have told your client *not* to make inappropriate use of his or her body, whether that involves standing on one leg, jangling loose pocket change, holding a hand over his or her mouth, or whatever, you can reverse the process and teach your client how to make *good* use of his or her body. This includes making appropriate eye contact, adopting a confident stance, using powerful gestures that are appropriate for the material and his or her intention in teaching, and so on.

Sensory Model of the World – Yesod – The Foundation

Assuming your client does not suffer from the above Real World issue, the next type of problem he or she might have is not having considered how the various pieces of the presentation puzzle fit together, including the needs of the audience. In other words, the client's Sensory Model of the World does not match with the audience's Sensory Model of the World, and the way the client presents the material will not match with his or her audience's needs.

Now, I'm not saying that people can't have both of these problems—a lack of Real World presentation skills and a failure to understand the audience's needs—at the same time. Of course they can. They could have no clue as to what the audience wants, and no clue how to provide it even if they do know what the audience wants. But let's take one step at a time.

You've checked that your client (let's say it's a woman) actually has reasonable presentation skills, or you've given her some skills training if she doesn't. It's time to check in on her internal model for presentations. Suppose you now ask her what her audience is there for, and she tells you she doesn't know. Some presenters simply teach whatever they know about a subject, without considering what their audience is actually there for and how they as a presenter can best fulfill the audience's needs. In short, they haven't considered their audience's map of the world.

Suppose your client is an engineer. She has good presentation skills and is able to explain a new solution to a complex engineering problem to a group of highly qualified engineers. Because she is so good at this type of presentation, she was asked to explain the company's new product to the board of directors. She went into the meeting quite prepared to explain the complex engineering issues involved and found the board totally disinterested in what she had to say.

In this situation, chances are that her view of the world and the board of directors' view the world are entirely different. The board of directors may be more interested in the launch date, the likely market size, and the profitability of the product, or the risks associated with product, than the engineering aspects. It's not that her presentation wasn't good; it's just that the Sensory Model of the World for the speaker is different from the Sensory Model of the World for the audience.

If you want to help your client with this sort of problem, you have to explain to her how different people have different models of the world. To become a more flexible presenter, she needs to consider her audience and how the material she is presenting fits in with their needs and with their Sensory Model of the World, not just with her Sensory Model of the World. Rather than being inside herself, tracking her own physical movements, she needs to step inside the audience.

Thoughts – Hod – Glory

Assuming your client does not suffer from either of the above issues, the next type of problem she might have is that she might be thinking inappropriate thoughts. This does not mean her thoughts are risqué; rather, her thoughts do not lead to the outcome she wants.

Assuming that the outcome she wants is for her audience to leave her presentation with one or two key ideas, or with a certain tool kit of skills, all of her thoughts should also be aligned with these outcomes. Unfortunately, it's natural for all sorts of other thoughts to intrude. For example, thoughts that can lead to the downfall of presenters include, "I'm not good enough. They won't want to listen to what I've got to say. They're judging me." If these thoughts, or some variation of them, are running around in the presenter's head, she will inevitably steer her presentation toward something that her audience does not want to listen to, simply to prove that her own unconscious prediction is true! It is likely to be a self-fulfilling prophecy.

If your client has this type of issue, your coaching will guide her to generate a new set of thoughts that supports her outcome. And as I've already discussed, her outcome should be her audience's outcome—what she wants for the audience. So she should think thoughts that "begin with the end in mind," meaning thoughts about her audience getting exactly what they need from her presentation.

And it is not simply important for her to have thoughts that are linked with the outcome; it's also important that she has these thoughts in the right way. I will be talking more about this later.

Emotion – Netzach – Eternity

Assuming that your client does not suffer from any of the above problems, the next problem she might have is one of feelings. For example, she may feel nervous or anxious when she has to speak in public.

Of course, in practice, the feelings that she has are likely to be influenced by the thoughts she has, and vice versa. There's no easy way to separate them. If she starts to think negative thoughts—"I'm not good enough. They won't want to listen to what I've got to say"—she will inevitably start to feel anxious. And if she begins to feel anxious, she's likely to question her own abilities; it's a chicken and egg situation.

Having said this, it is possible that your client simply feels bad whenever she sees or hears the trigger for the problem. For example, if she feels anxious when she has to speak in public, over time this can lead to the very sight of an audience acting as a trigger for her anxiety (based on the principles of classical conditioning).

So, separating thoughts and feelings from each other for a moment, if your client has the sort of issue in which she simply feels a negative emotion in a specific context, the coaching will revolve around teaching her how to access positive emotional states such as a feeling of confidence.

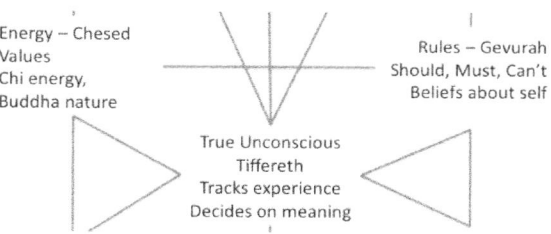

Energy – Chesed
Values
Chi energy,
Buddha nature

Rules – Gevurah
Should, Must, Can't
Beliefs about self

True Unconscious
Tiffereth
Tracks experience
Decides on meaning

True Unconscious – Tiferet – Beauty

To resolve the types of problems that are discussed above, your client needs to become aware of both her external sensory experience—especially the reactions of the audience as she speaks—and her own unconscious processes. This means that she needs to be aware of what she is seeing and hearing as well as her own physiology, her own emotions, and her own thoughts. This is not as easy as it sounds, and you will find that many of your clients are as blissfully unaware of the yawns of the audience as they are of the thoughts that are running through their heads, their gestures and physiology, their eye contact (or lack of eye contact) with the audience, and in some cases even the emotions they are feeling in their body.

Becoming aware of these unconscious internal processes, physiology, thoughts, and emotions, as well as the reactions of the audience, in real time will allow your client to make changes in her own behavior and physiology as well as her thoughts and feelings as she is giving the presentation.

However, it is not enough for her to simply be self-aware. She also has to make decisions and take action based on what is going on around her. To make these decisions, she has to make accurate and useful *meaning* out of what is happening around her. The way she does that is based upon her beliefs or internal rule book (which in turn is shaped by her education, cultural background, and so on), the values that are embedded in her physiology and emotions, her experiences, and her intuition.

Rules – Gevurah – Power

Assuming that your client does not suffer from any of the above problems (or that you have helped her to resolve them), the next problem she might have is one of belief. For example, she might believe that she's "not good enough."

Now, obviously if she does have this belief, the belief will begin to manifest itself in her thoughts. She may tell herself that she's not good enough and that the audience won't want to listen to what she has to say.

On the other hand, her belief may not manifest itself in her conscious thoughts; she may be able to suppress the thought yet still have the underlying unconscious belief. For example, research shows that unconscious beliefs about gender or racial stereotypes can adversely affect exam performance. Either way, if she holds a negative belief about herself, this is likely to sabotage her presentations. The coaching work would involve changing this belief using any one of a number of tools that are excellent for this purpose, such as the NLP belief change pattern, verbal reframing, EFT, and so on. Don't worry if you're not familiar with these; I will be talking about a few of them later on in the book.

Limiting beliefs may not be obvious, particularly if they result in a *lack* of feeling or a *lack* of a certain behavior (rather than a negative feeling or behavior). For example, I recently had a conversation with a young woman who told me that there was absolutely nothing interesting about her at all. You can imagine that when she held this limiting belief, she did not share anything about herself in conversation—after all, why would she when there was nothing interesting about her to share? When I pushed her a little to tell me what she did in her spare time, she told me about her bread-making skills and kept me entranced for twenty minutes explaining the leavening process and the difference between East Coast yeasts and West Coast yeasts.

Energy – Chesed – Mercy

Assuming your client does not suffer from any of the above problems, the next problem she might have is one of "energy." In Tree of Life Coaching, the concept of "energy" has many facets.

For example, energy can refer to what propels you through the world, i.e., your values. It may seem counterintuitive to think of values as energy; after all, and are they really words? Let's consider this for a moment: what is a value? In NLP, a value is defined as a word that creates a positive state. So, for example, if one person hears the word *freedom*, it may make him or her feel good, while the word *fairness* may not do anything for him or her. For another person, it may be the opposite; he or she feels energized and motivated by the concept of *fairness* but indifferent to the word *freedom*. The clash of these different values leads to much of the political dispute in the United States today. These values carry a lot of energy.

Perhaps you seek freedom. Maybe you desire money. You could pursue happiness or seek to generate love. Or perhaps equality and fairness are the things you value. Whatever values guide and motivate you, they also provide you with a certain type, or quality, of energy.

Let's take a couple of specific examples. You have a client whose main value is money; you might already know somebody like this. Much of his life will be focused around either acquiring money, spending money, or saving money. It's not that he is necessarily thinking about money all the time or experiencing some emotion about money; rather, it's that those thoughts or emotions will be generated whenever he is in a relevant context. For example, his "money value" drives him to feel desire whenever he sees something he wants to buy. Or perhaps it drives him to put money in his IRA. Or to spend most of his time at work in order to earn more money. Or perhaps it prevents him from being generous with his family, friends, or simply the waiter in the restaurant. Whatever it is, the money value acts as a bedrock or foundation for his thoughts and emotions, and therefore affects his behaviors.

Another client might have a very positive value, such as freedom. Again, this is not necessarily something she thinks about, or feels, all the time. However, it's the underlying bedrock that many of her thoughts and emotions are based on. Of course, how she thinks and feels and behaves as a result depends upon what type of freedom she values. One person may value freedom, and it leads her to choose a career where she is her own boss, with many people working for her, which "frees up" her time for more important things. But equally, her freedom value may lead her to choose a career where she has no responsibility, which "frees" her from the associated stress. Or her freedom value may have nothing to do with her career; it may simply lead her to choose adventure vacations in the mountains. Whatever type of freedom it is, it acts as an underlying energy for her—the bedrock of her thoughts, emotions, and behaviors.

Returning to your client with the fear of public speaking, the problem may be that she is not highly motivated to speak. In turn, this may be because she has not attached the idea of "public speaking" to her values—to the things that actually do motivate her. By exploring what's really important to her and why she's actually in the context where she is asked to speak in public in the first place, you can help her attach the *energy* of her values to the *behavior* of public speaking.

Chi Energy

Another type of Energy is the physical energy you generate in your body. In Southeast Asia, this is referred to as ki or chi energy—internal energy. You can generate internal energy using any one of a number of ancient practices such as chi kung, yoga, breathwork, or any sort of physical activity that moves the energy inside your body.

Chi kung generates and moves this internal energy by combining gentle movements and breathing with mental visualizations. These mental visualizations are similar to ones that may be used in NLP and hypnosis, such as the "backward spin" technique developed by Dr. Richard Bandler, the cofounder of NLP.

The Upper Triad

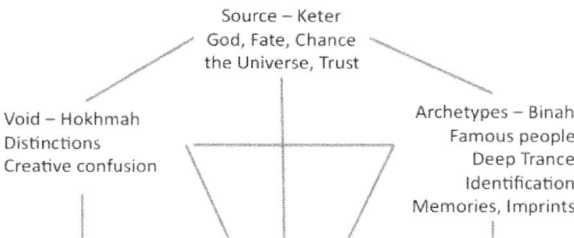

Source – Keter
God, Fate, Chance
the Universe, Trust

Void – Hokhmah
Distinctions
Creative confusion

Archetypes – Binah
Famous people
Deep Trance
Identification
Memories, Imprints

Archetypes – Binah – Understanding

Another type of problem that your public-speaking client might face relates to the archetypes that she holds in her life. Let's take an example:

Suppose your client says, "I'm not good enough." That's a belief that she holds about herself. Now, on one level, it doesn't really make a difference whether we call this a "belief" issue or an "archetypal" issue—it's still a limiting belief. In Tree of Life Coaching, the difference is that a limiting self-belief is something that you hold about yourself as an individual. Other people can do what you would like to be able to do but you can't.

In contrast, an archetypal belief is a belief that your client holds about herself because of the type or class of person she is. For example, if she says, "I'm not good enough—no one in my family ever graduated from college," this is archetypal in the sense that she is modeling herself and limiting herself based on other members of her family rather than on her own abilities. Similarly, somebody who limits herself because of her gender, race, or other shared characteristic has an archetypal problem. Or she may have a negative self-belief because her parents repeatedly told her that she was not good enough. Again, this belief is archetypal because it comes from a childhood imprint that she took from somebody else.

To assist your client with this issue, you need to provide her with a new "archetype" on which to model herself. You might do this, for example, using reimprinting. Reimprinting is based on the idea that we base our behavior on behavioral "imprints" that we obtain from our parents, caregivers, siblings, and other people who provide examples of "appropriate" behavior when we are very young. We take these examples and internalize them, and then we replicate these behaviors in our own life. This is actually a great way to learn when you model yourself on people who are resourceful. However, if you grow up surrounded by role models who are themselves unresourceful (for example, alcoholic parents), or if you grow up in an abusive home, you might internalize these unresourceful and negative behaviors.

Using reimprinting, we can lead the client to "gift" new resources to her childhood models so that the models themselves become more resourceful (at least in the client's memory). Therefore, their imprints become more resourceful, and the client also becomes more resourceful.

New archetypes can also be provided using Deep Trance Identification (DTI). DTI uses this natural imprinting process to allow the client to take on the behavioral imprint of their ideal role model. (You can find out more about Deep Trance Identification in *Deep Trance Identification* by Shawn Carson and Jess Marion with John Overdurf.)

The Void – Hokhmah – Wisdom

The Void refers to that part of the Tree of Life that exists before "differentiations" are made and that leads to these original differentiations. If you want to get philosophical, Wisdom is the state of the universe as, or just before, it splits into yin and yang, male and female, good and bad, possible and impossible, and so on.

Differentiations can lead to problems. For example, any judgment is a differentiation: "This thing is good, and that thing is bad." It is quite likely that your client—the one with the fear of public speaking—is imagining the audience making such a judgment, and in this case the judgment is about her, the speaker. Typically, a client with a fear of public speaking feels that she is being judged.

Once we make a distinction or a decision, we stop learning because we already "know." People who already "know everything" are not able to recreate themselves. In order to reverse the judgment your client has made, or the judgment that your client believes the audience is making, we have to return to Wisdom.

Within Wisdom, anything is possible because the world can then be split in a different way, and the impossible becomes possible. Entering Wisdom, and being able to lead your clients into Wisdom, is a key part of Tree of Life Coaching and one that I will be returning to in Chapter 24.

The Source – Kether – The Crown

The Source is the final point in the Tree of Life. It represents the source of all life and all creative energy in the universe. If you are religious, it might refer to God or the point at which God enters our universe. If you're not religious but you are spiritual, it may represent the source of spiritual energy in the universe. If you're neither religious nor spiritual, the Source may represent the Big Bang—the physical, scientific birth of the universe—or it may represents the quantum wave of the universe that creates unexpected events in our lives. Or it may simply represent the hand of fate or chance.

In Tree of Life Coaching, the Source represents the energy that sends us in a new and unexpected direction. It could be a flash of inspiration, a sickness that causes us to reevaluate our lives, a remarkable person we meet, or any other synchronicity that throws us off the track we thought we were on and in a new direction.

I explain in detail how to ascend, and then descend, the Tree of Life in later chapters. At this stage, I will simply say that once you've reached Wisdom or the Source, you're able to find the ideal and perfect resource to rebalance your Tree of Life. As you descend the Tree, you can use this resource to rebalance each branch of the Tree, creating a new and healthier reality for yourself.

In the next chapter, we will consider how modern scientific knowledge about the brain-body system supports the Tree of Life model.

Chapter 3: The Neuroscience of the Tree of Life

Here at Changing Mind Publishing, we often include a chapter on neuroscience in our books, and this one is no exception. This doesn't mean to say that neuroscientists are researching the Tree of Life, because as far as we know, they're not. However, neuroscience is providing many tantalizing clues that hint at how and why certain coaching techniques and other change-work tools can help clients resolve their problems and better deal with the world around them.

Another great reason to include a discussion of neuroscience is that psychological research indicates that basing a conclusion on neuroscience makes it much more believable than if the same conclusion is based purely on psychology! We are therefore strong believers in providing our clients with neuroscientific explanations for what we are asking them to do and how it will help them change. Therefore, you can think of this chapter as providing you, as the coach, with a set of metaphors that you can use with clients to reinforce what you are doing when you use Tree of Life Coaching with them.

Western science is traditionally "reductionist"—meaning it seeks to break things down into small parts, determine how each part works, and then reassemble the parts back into the whole. This is very different from Eastern thinking, which tends to view things more holistically, as an irreducible whole. The Tree of Life comes from an

Eastern tradition rather than a Western tradition. Although the Tree of Life contains ten different branches, it also contains pathways that link these branches to each other. These pathways do not carry energy only in one direction, but rather in both directions. As a result, you can't understand the Tree of Life except as a holistic system of experience. So although we will be considering individual branches in the course of our examination of the Tree of Life, any branch only makes sense as part of the whole Tree of Life.

Neuroscience arises out of the Western medical tradition. As such, neuroscientists have traditionally asked the question, "What does this part of the brain do?" The way to answer this question historically was to find a person who had some kind of mental defect, wait until he or she died, and then do an autopsy on his or her brain. If a portion of the brain was damaged, there was a good chance that the damaged part of the brain was responsible for whatever function or activity the person had had a problem with in life. For example, by performing autopsies on people who had problems understanding speech or forming meaningful sentences, neuroscientists were able to identify the parts of the brain responsible for speech—Broca's area and Wernicke's area.

As neuroscience advanced, scientists were able to carry out experiments on living creatures. At first, these experiments could only be carried out on animals or occasionally on human beings who were undergoing brain surgery. Experimenting on the brains of live human subjects was considered unethical (strangely, experimenting on the brains of live animals is considered ethical in scientific circles!). But then, with the advent of brain scanning technologies, especially fMRI, experiments could be carried out on live, healthy human beings. By asking subjects to perform a specific action or undertake a specific mental activity, scientists could literally look inside their brain as it was working.

As a result of the recent research that is being carried out using fMRIs and other brain scanning technology, we now know far more about how the brain works than we did even thirty years ago. Our knowledge may still be sketchy, but certain processes are becoming a lot clearer. Most of the neuroscience research still focuses on the function of specific brain areas, but we are starting to see a much more nuanced and holistic view, not just of the *brain* as one complete system but also of the brain and body as one system.

Traditional Western Mechanistic Paradigm

Here are a few examples to show you what I mean when I say that Western science is reductionist. The model or paradigm that was traditionally used for a human being was that of a top-down system, a machine, in which the brain acts as the control center, and the body responds to the brain's commands. In this paradigm, emotions become almost unnecessary; the brain is responsible for moving the body by first making a decision using the prefrontal cortex (the executive brain), which sends a message to the motor cortex, which in turn sends messages to the muscles to contract or relax, allowing the body to move.

These messages that are sent from the prefrontal cortex to other parts of the brain travel from neuron to neuron through electrochemical action in the synapses. The brain becomes a sort of supercomputer, with the neurons being the wiring.

Within this paradigm, the brain is also responsible for creating emotions in the body. The mechanisms whereby thoughts generate the release of hormones and other chemicals that regulate emotion are quite well understood. These emotional responses allow the body to react in more nuanced ways, for example, speeding up the heart rate and diverting blood to the major muscle groups when the body is experiencing fear ("fight, flight or freeze").

If you were to sketch out this paradigm as a picture, you might have the conscious executive brain on the top and the unconscious mind underneath. Under the executive brain, within the unconscious, you would show the motor cortex. The motor cortex would be shown receiving instruction from the executive brain, and the muscles of the body would be shown receiving signals from the motor cortex. Within the unconscious brain, you would show the "emotional brain" (including "parts" such as the amygdala and hypothalamus). The emotional brain would be shown sending messages to the thyroid and other glands in the body, which in turn would send messages to the heart, lungs, and other organs.

Holistic Paradigm

Of course, even the Western mechanistic paradigm of the human experience recognizes certain feedback loops. So, for example, the executive brain sends instructions to the motor cortex, which triggers the muscles that allow the body to move. However, the movements of the body are sensed by various sensory systems, such as our sense of balance, and relayed back to the brain.

But the more we learn about how the brain and body work, the more we realize it's not simply, or even primarily, a top-down system with a few feedback loops. Instead, it's a cybernetic system in which each part shares information with, and directly or indirectly influences (but does not necessarily control), every other part. For example, the physiology of the body is partially responsible for creating (or at least influencing) emotions in the body.

Recent research has demonstrated that the posture of the body and the gestures you make not only generate certain emotional states, such as confidence and determination, but your physiology can actually stimulate the production of hormones. The body is not simply controlled by the brain—to a certain extent, the brain is controlled by the body.

The body is also responsible for "creating" emotions in the brain just as much as the brain is responsible for generating emotions in the body. Emotions that you experience in your *head* (rather than in your body) are partially the reflection of signals sent back from the body. Your body literally tells your brain what you're feeling.

Although specific parts of the brain specialize in specific functions, all mental functions involve activation of numerous "parts" of the brain. It's just not possible to accurately say, "This part of the brain does function X," because for X to happen, many different areas of the brain need to work together. Although the firing of individual neurons is, of course, very important in terms of brain function, the brain also operates on a more holistic basis using brainwave frequencies that are strung across wider areas of the brain than just individual neurons.

It's no longer possible to describe the activity of the human brain, or the brain and body, according to a mechanistic cause-and-effect model. The human brain and body form a web of flowing and interacting energies that can manifest actions, thoughts, and behaviors in unexpected ways. This is exactly the sort of web of interaction that we actually see when we look at the Tree of Life model. Within the Tree of Life is the potential for effect-cause as well as cause-effect!

Let's consider the Tree of Life from the point of view of neuroscience. As before, we will start at the bottom in the Real World.

The Real World – Malkuth – The Kingdom

The Real World represents the body and the physical structure of the brain. Your body and brain have chemical and physical processes that allow you to digest food, release the calorific energy in that food, and convert that energy into movement, heat, and so on. In addition, your physical body interacts with the physical world around it.

This is equivalent to the traditional Western paradigm of the brain and body as a machine. While this view is correct and extremely useful in many contexts, it's not the only possible or useful perspective.

Sensory Model of the World – Yesod – Foundation

Although your body and brain physically exist in the Real World, you have no direct experience of the Real World. Instead, various types of energy flow in from the Real World and are captured by your senses.

This energy might be electromagnetic energy in the form of light, or pressure waves in the form of sound, or chemically active particles in the form of smell and taste, or pressure and temperature in the form of touch.

In this perspective of the brain-body, the senses become measurement devices that take in information from the Real World. This information is processed largely according to predetermined heuristics and models of meaning. Some of these heuristics are hardwired according to our DNA, and some are learned in childhood or later in life. The resulting meaning is then translated into action (behavior). So while traditional Western paradigms have historically treated the mind-body either as a top-down system controlled by the executive brain and emotional brain, or as a complex electrochemical machine, this new paradigm treats a human being as essentially a tool for measuring various signals from the outside world and turning those signals into responsive behaviors.

According to this paradigm, a human being doesn't experience the world around him or her. Rather, the senses seek to estimate certain key variables that will be useful in generating appropriate behaviors. Your experience comes through your senses and is distorted in all sorts of ways as your brain creates the virtual reality that we call "reality." To take just one example, if you rap your knuckles on a table or other surface, you will see the impact, hear the impact, and feel the impact. Each of these sensory signals travels to your brain at a different speed and is then processed at a different speed. However, you will likely experience all three as taking place at the same time; your brain adjusts its own *sensory* time to make it seem that the sight, sound, and feeling occur simultaneously. Your brain does this, presumably, because it wants you to understand that these represent the "same event" in the Real World. It seems that the human brain is invested in making all virtual reality as real as possible!

Not only do our senses distort reality, but we're also actually not aware of the vast majority of the sensory experience we have. A great example of this is the sense of smell. You will probably be aware of the smell of coffee when you walk into Starbucks, but did you know that your unconscious mind is also paying attention to the smells of the people around you to let you know whether they are healthy or sick, angry or calm, even whether they would be a good life partner for you? In fact, so important is your sense of smell to the relationships you have with other people that after you shake somebody's hand, research shows that you will unconsciously sniff the palm of your own hand in order to pick up the other person's scent!

Now, in one way, your senses do indeed provide you with a pretty accurate map of the Real World. After all, you are probably able to walk around your house or apartment without bumping into furniture! But sometimes our senses operate purely in our Sensory Model of the World and seem to create an internal experience that has nothing to do with reality. An obvious example of this is somebody who has a phobia—perhaps a phobia of something that isn't even dangerous, but each time the person encounters it, he or she goes into a "fight, flight or freeze" reaction.

Another example of senses being more about your model of the world than the Real World comes from classical conditioning (stimulus-response). Classical conditioning pairs a stimulus from the Real World, such as the ringing of a bell, with an internal experience, such as salivation. Of course, the best-known example is Pavlov pairing the ringing of a bell with feeding time for his dogs, until simply ringing the bell would make the dogs salivate, even if no food was offered to them. Following this conditioning, their response to the ringing of the bell took place within their Sensory Model of the World (where it was associated with food) rather than in the Real World (where no food was present).

Thoughts – Hod – Glory

With Thoughts, we return to another of the Western paradigms. In this paradigm, the executive brain sits like the Wizard of Oz behind the curtain, putting on a performance of controlling everything that's going on. Unfortunately for this Wizard, neuroscience indicates that the potential for thought arises from a complex blend of external stimuli and internal programming rather than an all-wise intelligence that inhabits our brain. Like the Wizard of Oz, our thoughts are often at the mercy of events rather than driving events.

There's a movie called *Up* in which there are super-intelligent talking dogs. However, intelligent as these dogs are, each time they see a squirrel, they turn around and say, "Squirrel!" This is how the human brain works as well; when something in the Real World catches our attention, it stimulates a thought about that thing. If our brains are sufficiently stimulated, that thought pops into our conscious awareness.

But even if such thoughts don't have enough energy to come into conscious awareness, they can still be there. A great example of this is the psychological process called "priming." Priming is when you see or hear something in the outside world, and it stimulates thoughts inside your mind but at such a low level that you're not consciously aware of it happening.

A lot of research has been done on priming. For example, in one study, people were asked to complete word search puzzles. In the control group the puzzles simply had random words, but in the experimental group the puzzles included words that had a subtle connection with aging—words such as *Florida* (which, in the United States, is often associated with retirement). The participants in the study were filmed walking along a corridor to and from the room where the experiment took place, and the time it took them to walk up and then down the corridor was measured. The researchers found that the participants who had been "primed" with the "aging" words took longer to walk down the corridor after completing the quiz than they did walking up the corridor before the quiz, while in the control group the times were roughly the same. What this shows is that simply being exposed to this set of "aging" words impacted them not just mentally but also physically.

In terms of the Tree of Life, this experiment shows that information or energy flowed from the outside world in the form of the puzzles, passing through the participants' map of the world (where, for example, *Florida* means "retirement") and into the thoughts of the participants, and then flowing from those thoughts into the bodies, and hence the actions, of the participants. Once again, this demonstrates the subtle web of connections between the various points on the Tree of Life.

Emotion – Netzach – Eternity

Emotions often begin as thoughts. We think about something, and it makes us feel a certain way. But what is the purpose of these emotions, and how do they arise? It turns out that these are surprisingly deep and difficult questions to answer.

Emotions are generated in the limbic system of the brain (the "emotional brain"), which is a very old part of the brain. The limbic system is connected to the frontal cortex (the executive brain), which allows you to "know" what you are feeling and, more importantly, allows you to control your feelings using your conscious mind.

The limbic system contains the hypothalamus, which in turn is linked to the pituitary gland. The hypothalamus and pituitary glands produce the hormones that lead to your physical response to emotion, such as increased heart rate, increased blood flow to your muscles, and so on.

An important part of your emotional response is generated by the amygdala. The amygdala monitors incoming sensory information, for example, from your eyes, and prepares you for an appropriate emotional response even before that signal has been consciously processed. If you have ever been walking down a dark street and jumped out of your skin because you saw something moving at your feet (even before you realized it was just a paper bag blowing in the wind), you have your amygdala to thank.

49

Emotions arise in one hemisphere of the brain or the other. Many negative emotions originate in the right brain, which seems to have a much darker view of life than the left brain! In whichever side of the brain it arises, the emotional signal is then shared between the two hemispheres of the brain through the corpus callosum. If the signal isn't fully shared between right brain and left brain, you might have an emotional response (in the right brain) without knowing (in the left brain) exactly what you are feeling or why.

The emotion is also communicated to the hippocampus, which is involved in the encoding and retrieval of memories. The more emotional a particular experience is, the more likely that it will be remembered.

It is important to note that most emotions are extremely transitory. In fact, we talk about the "90-second rule" that says an emotion typically lasts no more than 90 seconds unless we do something to maintain it. Of course, if we review the events that initially caused the emotion in our mind and relive the experience, we can keep the emotion going indefinitely.

Obviously, some emotions tend to last for much longer, such as depression. These become part of the Energy branch of the Tree of Life, which is discussed below.

The True Unconscious – Tiferet – Beauty

Your unconscious mind does many things. It keeps your heart beating, keeps you breathing at night, and instructs your stomach to digest food. We are going to ignore these basic physiological tasks, or perhaps it would be more accurate to say that we will consider them to be part of the Real World. Instead, when talking about your unconscious, we will focus on the part that monitors, and then makes sense of, the world around you, including your own body and physiological responses.

Your brain has many different mechanisms designed to monitor your experience. The insights your brain obtains from these mechanisms are not necessarily shared with your conscious mind. For example, in the section above on emotions, I talked about the role of the amygdala in monitoring incoming sensory information for emotional content. The role of the amygdala is to "prime," or prepare, the brain for the incoming information so you can react faster to threats and opportunities. It's as if the amygdala is saying, "Get ready—there is some important information coming through!"

Your brain may respond to these incoming messages by redirecting your senses toward the source of the stimulus that's generating the message that is deemed to be important. For example, if you hear a loud noise, your brain will automatically direct your eyes in the direction of the sound to identify its source; you've heard it, and now you get to see it. This allows your brain to gather even more information about these important external events.

Other parts of your brain are designed to monitor internal processes and make sense of the world around you. For example, if somebody asked you the way to the park, your brain will begin to access memories of going to the park so that you can answer the question, or perhaps will access a more abstract mental map of where the park is or even a value judgment about whether or not it's a good idea for the person to go to the park. In the context of your client who has a fear of speaking in public, she sees the eyes of the audience upon her, and her brain creates the meaning that she is being judged.

In any case, what's really important to understand is that your brain is monitoring far more information, both internal and external, than you are consciously aware of. Your True Unconscious is doing this monitoring. Your True Unconscious then makes sense of this information to guide your future actions.

Rules – Gevurah – Power

You may be surprised to learn that human beings do not have the largest brains in the animal kingdom. Although the human brain is disproportionately large compared to our body size, our brains are actually quite small compared to those of certain other animals, such as whales, elephants, and even dolphins. But the human brain differs in processing power from those of other animals thanks to the size of our neocortex.

So what is the neocortex, and what does it do? The human brain is sometimes described as an *association machine*, or an abstraction machine. It seems that one of the traits that sets us apart from other animals is our ability to make connections between two or more different events. This ability to associate several events, and to abstract those events into a more generalized meaning, appears to take place largely in the neocortex. In fact, the neocortex seems to be specifically designed to make these types of abstractions.

Generalizations are built up in the neocortex, based upon all observations and interactions with the world around us, through a process of induction. Induction involves taking a number of observations and coming up with a general rule or principle from those observations. For example, before the discovery of Australia, Europeans believed that all swans were white. After all, no European had ever seen a swan that was not white until they visited Australia and discovered black swans. These generalizations are examples of belief.

There are many different types of belief; for example, there are factual beliefs about the color of swans and other facts about the world, independent of my existence within it. Europeans may have been surprised to discover that their belief about all swans being white was wrong, but it was unlikely to change anybody's life.

There are also beliefs about my place in the world, for example, that I'm an excellent coach. There are also beliefs about how the world should be; for example, I know that I *have* to finish this manuscript because my business partner wants to send it to the publisher, and that I shouldn't eat with my mouth open because it's rude. And there are beliefs about how the world has to be; for example, I know it's a bad idea to throw my computer out of the window because if I do, gravity will accelerate it toward the ground at a rate of 9.8 meters per second squared, and it's going to break as soon as it hits the ground!

So some of these beliefs revolve around how things are, the color of swans, and the existence of gravity. But others revolve around me and my behaviors, what I can and can't do because I'm good or bad at them, what I have to do or not do because somebody expects me to, or because I expect myself to, or because society expects me to. It's these abstractions, encoded in your neocortex, that tell you what you can and can't, have to or mustn't, should or shouldn't do, that we're interested in when we talk about Rules.

Energy – Chesed – Mercy

In the section above, I talked about the special ability that human beings have to generalize, and to abstract, using the neocortex. Sometimes these abstractions become separated from a real situation or context.

So, for example, I might say to you, "I have to help Fred paint his house." Notice I'm not saying, "I offered to help Fred paint his house" or "I'm going to help Fred paint his house"—I'm saying I *have to*. When you ask me why, I tell you that Fred helped me repair my roof. You probe further and discover that there was no agreement between Fred and me that he would help me repair my roof and I would help him paint his house, yet I still *have* to. When you hear this sort of language, you note that there is something underlying this "have to"—a duty to return a favor, or a value or friendship or reciprocity, or something similar.

These duties, these values, exist independently of any specific context. If I have a value of friendship, it exists independently of the friends I have; I could even move to a new country where I have no friends and still value friendship. And the reason it can exist in this kind of vacuum is because it has an emotional attachment for me; when I think of friendship, I feel good.

There are other types of "feelings'" that become hardwired into us. These are emotions that we feel on such a regular basis that the neural pathways to triggering these emotions become "superhighways." For example, you might know somebody who's always happy (or always depressed, or always optimistic). That person might not be happy right now, but we know that he or she could burst into laughter at any moment; it becomes the person's "Buddha-nature." These types of commonly felt emotions become much easier to trigger within that individual's brain than others. Because of this, we are including these in the branch of Energy in the Tree of Life.

Archetypes – Binah – Understanding

As we discussed above, the Western discipline of neuroscience tends to take a reductionist view of the brain, asking what each part of the brain does as a separate functional element. The more holistic operation of the brain is perhaps not as well understood.

It does appear, however, that the human brain is able to integrate many different ideas, principles, and experiences into a whole. For example, if you think about a specific person, you're probably able to see his face, hear his voice, remember certain times and places where you were with him, and also appreciate his beliefs and values, and have a sense of him as a person. This requires your brain to be able to integrate and coordinate many different ideas that you have about a person. The author Douglas Hofstadter describes this as a Strange Loop.

Although is not clear exactly how the human brain is able to do this (at least I have not seen any research that explains it), nevertheless this is what we are talking about when we talk about Archetypes. An

Archetype is a set of characteristics that are linked in the brain to form a coherent whole.

The Void – Hokhmah – Wisdom

When you were born, your experience was seamless. You didn't distinguish what you saw from what you heard or what you felt. You couldn't tell where one object ended and another one began. You had no frame of reference to make these distinctions. But then something happened; probably shortly after your birth, an object appeared in your visual field, together with a touch and a smell, that had meaning, and that meaning generated a feeling of safety. And on one level you understood that meaning, even though you couldn't explain what the meaning was because you didn't yet know the word *mother*.

Your life is spent making distinctions about the world around you. You look at something and it becomes the "foreground" of your attention, and everything else moves into the "background."

Your brain has a kind of spotlight of attention that it shines on one piece of your experience. In fact, research shows that not only are you not very good at multitasking, but you actually can't multitask. Even when you try to multitask, you simply end up putting your attention on one thing, then another, then the first thing, then the second, in a repeating cycle.

We get stuck—stuck in ruts, stuck in a problem—when we begin to make the same distinctions over and over again. If you always do what you've always done, you'll always get what you always got. Returning to the origin of these distinctions, Wisdom, allows you to begin to make new distinctions for your experiences, and find new solutions to your problems.

The Source – Kether – The Crown

No matter how well your system is working, how well you are able to pay attention to the world around you, how sophisticated your thoughts, how resourceful your emotions, how supportive your beliefs, how aligned your values, how powerful your archetypes, and how adept you are at making distinctions, you can experience sudden and unexpected changes.

When you have the flexibility to adapt to these changes, you have something that is called resiliency. Resiliency represents the ability of your brain to rewire itself based upon the situation in which you find yourself. This rewiring of the brain is known as neuroplasticity. When your brain is able to rapidly rewire itself to changing circumstances, we say that you have resiliency.

Chapter 4: The Three Coaching Paradigms

We can break coaching down into three different paradigms, depending upon where the principal focus of the coach is. I will discuss each in turn.

The first coaching paradigm is client-centered coaching. In client-centered coaching, the focus is on the client as an individual, and the coaching revolves around the specific techniques the coach might select in order to offer that individual client the experiences he or she needs in order to make the desired change. Each client is treated differently, and there is no one-size-fits-all philosophy—far from it.

The second coaching paradigm uses one or more protocols to help the client achieve the change he or she desires. For example, when my colleagues and I (at our hypnosis center in New York) are helping clients quit smoking, we base our work around a specific protocol we have developed that is specifically aimed at smokers (by the way, if you're interested, you can find our protocol in our book *QUIT: The Hypnotist's Handbook to Running Effective Stop Smoking Sessions*).

The third and final coaching paradigm focuses on one specific coaching modality, or one specific technique, that is then applied to all clients. For example, some hypnotists might use deep trance coupled with direct suggestion for all their clients, while other hypnotists might use a script book for all clients. Some change workers might only use EFT, or just NLP, or whatever.

Although I am breaking coaching down into three different paradigms, it's very rare to find a coach who works exclusively in only one of these paradigms. For example, we use a protocol for smoking cessation, but because we've been trained in a more client-centric method of coaching, even when we're using our stop-smoking protocol, we still tailor it to the needs of the specific client. So even though we are using a protocol, by tailoring it to the specific needs of the client, we are also using a client-centric approach. Similarly, somebody who uses the deep trance and direct suggestion approach is likely to use his or her skills and experience to tailor those suggestions to the client-centric needs of the individual he or she is working with.

Likewise, someone who uses one specific coaching modality, such as EFT, may well use different protocols within that modality depending upon the presenting issue. And the coach will also use his or her skills and experience to tailor the sessions to the client-centric needs of the individual he or she is working with.

So, any coach is likely to use some combination of the three paradigms. However, he or she is likely to put more weight or focus on one of the paradigms than the others.

Applying Tree of Life Coaching

The wonderful thing about Tree of Life Coaching is that it can be applied to any of these coaching paradigms. What do I mean by this?

Client-centric Tree of Life Coaching

How can we apply the client-centric approach to coaching? This begs the question, how do we, as coaches, know precisely what an individual client's needs are? In other words, how do we find out enough about the client to know what tools or techniques to use? This is where the Tree of Life becomes extremely useful.

You see, we can use the Tree of Life as a diagnostic coaching tool that allows us to uncover the way the client currently organizes his or her experience, and therefore to come up with the most effective way to help the client. Once again, for the sake of clarity, I will point out that I am using the word *diagnostic* in its common everyday usage, meaning to discover a characteristic, not in a medical sense (you cannot attempt to diagnose a medical condition unless you are medically qualified).

Using the Tree of Life, we coaches can discover whether a client's problem arises from a "faulty" map of the world that is no longer serving him, or from thoughts that are running around in his mind, or from emotions he is feeling in the body, or from beliefs and other rules that he tries to follow, or from values that no longer serve him (such as "away from" values or "clashing" values), or from troubling memories or inappropriate role models, or from an inability to creatively generate new options in life, or from a combination of these, or from something beyond even these.

I will talk about how to use the Tree of Life as a diagnostic coaching tool later in this book.

Using the Tree of Life to Construct Amazingly Effective Protocols

Once you have a little bit of experience in the coaching field, it is pretty easy to build a protocol to address a specific issue, whether it's smoking cessation, performance anxiety, weight loss, or whatever. The question is how effective a specific protocol will be in addressing the issue it is aimed at and how it can be improved to make it more effective.

Many factors go into the effectiveness of a specific protocol, the most important one being the level of rapport between the coach and client, but also the skill and experience of the coach, the motivation of the client, and the tools and techniques that are brought to bear in changing the client's experience away from his problem and into his outcome.

The Tree of Life can be used to assemble the optimal set of tools and techniques within the specific protocol by making sure that the protocol visits each of the branches of the Tree of Life and makes whatever changes are required to resolve the issue, or the part of the issue that lies along that branch. For example, any good protocol will address the thoughts the client has when engaging or about to engage in the problem behavior or when about to feel the problem state or feeling.

Later, as an example, I will show you how to do this, using our stop smoking protocol as an example.

Using the Tree of Life within Your Coaching Modality

You may be the sort of coach who uses a lot of different techniques, drawing from the hypnosis, NLP, EFT, Clean Language, provocative therapy, or any of the other amazing coaching modalities that are out there. On the other hand, you may like to focus on one modality and become completely masterful at that. Perhaps you only use classical hypnosis, or you're an EFT Master, a Clean Language facilitator, or you swear by the power of NLP.

If you do work wholly or mainly within one modality, the Tree of Life can offer you a wonderful resource to use within that modality, whatever it might be. Any client experience, including a problem, can be analyzed using the Tree of Life. The Tree of Life allows you to understand how your client has modeled his or her world and what he or she is thinking and feeling, as well as his or her book of rules, views, and archetypal experiences. You can then use your specific modality to change any (or all) of these branches that are involved in creating or maintaining the problem.

Chapter 5: Using the Tree of Life in Client Centered Coaching

Everyone has his or her own unique Tree of Life.

In addition, you don't only have one Tree of Life—you have a different Tree of Life for every different context in which you live as a human being. You have one Tree of Life for when you are a coach, another for when you are a husband, wife, girlfriend, or boyfriend, another for when you are a parent, another for when you are a friend, and so on.

You could even argue that you have a separate Tree of Life for every *moment* of your existence. After all, we are always changing. Our thoughts are changing, our emotions are changing, our rules and values are changing, and we accumulate new archetypal reference experiences. Sometimes your Tree of Life changes slowly, like a tree going through the cycles of the seasons. Sometimes your Tree of Life changes quickly, as if struck by a bolt of lightning, which allows another tree to grow in its place.

Whenever you have an experience in the world, there is a Tree of Life associated with that specific experience:

- The experience takes place in a Real World context.
- Within that Real World context, certain events or actions are "causing" certain results or outcomes. And certain Real World

events are taken to have meaning, and those meanings are causing other outcomes. As a result, you're paying attention to certain aspects of what's going on around you. And you're not paying attention to other aspects.

- You are thinking certain thoughts. These may be in the form of internal dialogue or pictures and movies.
- You're feeling certain feelings.
- You're believing certain things about yourself and the world around you. You might believe there are things you can and can't do, or should and shouldn't do, or must and mustn't do. You might not be aware of these beliefs, and yet they are nevertheless influencing you. You may believe that your beliefs stay constant at least over the short term, but in fact they don't. The more positive you're feeling in the moment, the more positive your beliefs about yourself are likely to be, and vice versa.
- You're valuing certain things. Again, you may or may not be aware of these values, yet they will be influencing you whether or not you are aware of them. Again, you may think that the things you value remain constant, at least over the short term, but you'd be wrong. In times of stress and danger, we often value safety more than we do in times of peace, while if you are feeling confident, you might value adventure more. Your values are dependent on your state of mind at the moment.
- You have access to certain archetypes, archetypal experiences, and memories. But the archetypes you have access to will not be the same across every context. The ones that are most likely to be activated are those that relate to the particular situation you are in, so that if you visit the zoo, you're more likely to remember other times in the past when you went to the zoo (rather than times when you played basketball, for example). This is referred to as "state-dependent learning."
- You also have the potential for pure creativity. The potential for creativity is also not the same across all contexts, and the things that arise out of Wisdom are different—once again, depending upon how you're feeling and your state of mind.

The same is true of your client, whether he is deep in his problem or in his most resourceful state. By understanding his Tree of Life when he is in his problem, you better understand the problem. And understanding his Tree of Life when he is at his most resourceful lets you, as the coach, show him how to access this resourceful state at will.

When your client comes to you with a problem, it is because his Tree of Life has not yet adapted appropriately to the Real World context in which he finds himself. In the coaching context, once you have found your client's Tree of Life in the moments in which he experiences his problem, it is time for you, as the coach, to help him grow a new Tree of Life—one that will support him, nurture him, and shelter him. So Tree of Life Coaching involves providing your client with a resourceful Tree of Life *in the specific context he wants to change.* This might involve cutting down his current Tree of Life in order to replace it with another, more resourceful Tree of Life. This resourceful Tree of Life may be one that he has access to at other times in his life, or it may be one that you help him plant and nurture from a seed.

You can grow a new Tree of Life from any one of the branches. For example, you may offer your client a simple reframe of a thought that he is thinking in his problem state. This reframe may lead to a new way of thinking and new thoughts. These new thoughts may in turn lead to new feelings and new behaviors. Thinking, feeling, and behaving in a new way can begin to build new beliefs about what is possible and new values about what is important, which can blossom into new archetypes and new potentialities.

On the other hand, a change in the Tree of Life may appear suddenly and spontaneously, seemingly out of nowhere, appearing fully formed from Wisdom—St. Paul seeing the light on the road to Damascus, perhaps. This sudden change can then cascade through your client's entire being, changing everything he believes, everything that is important to him, his thoughts and values, and the Real World context where he decides to spend his time.

Remember that your client's Tree of Life will always organize itself to be internally consistent. This can be good if a positive change cascades through the rest of the Tree of Life. However, if your client begins to think positive thoughts about the problem context, but nevertheless is feeling negative emotions and has an unresourceful physiology, the negative emotions and physiology may quickly overwhelm the positive thought.

So as a coach, you have to be ready to seize upon any positive change that your client makes, whether it is a new feeling, a different way of thinking about things, a new belief, a new value, a new insight, or simply a change in physiology. When you seize this change, you need to hold it and protect it while it begins to spread through the client's Tree of Life.

The Quantum Zeno Effect

The quantum Zeno effect is a principle of quantum physics that also applies in psychology. It stands for the principle that "a watched pot never boils," meaning that the more we pay attention to something, the more it tends to stay the same. In the context of physics, the Quantum Zeno effect was identified while scientists were observing the decay of radioactive particles. The rate at which these particles decayed should have been random; however, the scientists found that the more times they measured the state of the particles, the longer it took the particles to decay. The act of observation itself tended to maintain the current state of the particles.

The same principle applies on a psychological level. For example, if your client has a fear of flying, the more times he thinks about his fear or tells people about his fear, the more fixed the fear becomes. On the other hand, if he focuses his attention on something apart from the fear, especially how he would like to be instead, the fear will tend to naturally dissipate.

This is an important principle in Tree of Life Coaching. It means that when you're coaching a client and you see or hear a shift in some

64

aspect of his Tree of Life that moves him out of the problem, especially if it moves him into a positive place, you should immediately begin to focus your client's attention on that change. By fixing his attention on the positive change, the quantum Zeno effect will tend to keep that positive change in place while allowing any residual negative parts of his Tree of Life to dissipate.

And when these negative aspects dissipate, they will tend to be replaced by something more positive arising from the first positive change he made.

Let's consider a simple example. You have a client who came to see you because he has a fear of flying.

Coach: What do you want to work through?

Client: I have to go on a business trip to the West Coast, and I'm terrified of flying.

[The client immediately clenches his fists, and his spine becomes tense. The coach now knows what the client looks like in the Real World context because the client has just imagined being there! This saves the coach from having to associate the client into the "last time and place."]

Coach: I see that. How do you know it's time to be afraid?

Client: [Looking up to the left] I don't know—I'm just scared!

Coach: What picture do you see when you look up there [pointing up to the client's left]?

Client: Oh, I guess I'm seeing a plane crashing. Isn't that funny…

Coach: Well, it's not funny, but it would certainly explain how you're making yourself feel scared! [The coach forces the client to take responsibility for his own state.]

Let me ask you this: why is it important to you to go on this business trip? [The coach is looking for a positive value in the Energy branch of the Tree of Life.]

Client: I'm meeting with investors; I need them to invest in my company if it's going to be a success.

Coach: And what's important about your company being a success? [Searching for more values]

CLent: We have this new technology that could transform the lives of people in the Third World and really help them out!

[The client lights up as he says this. He has moved from a value of "safety" in fearing to fly, to a value of making life better for people. Keeping the client's attention on this new "bud" on the Tree of Life can make the change work much more easily. The coach begins by bringing the client's attention to the new bud and then by bringing this change down into the branch of Emotions, where it becomes felt in the body.]

Coach: So you'll be transforming people's lives—that's great! How you feel about that?

Client: It's great! I feel fantastic about it. It's like joy!

Coach: That's great! Where do you feel that joy in your body?

Client: It's in my chest. I guess it's in my heart.

Coach: When you're transforming people's lives and you feel that joy in your heart, what are you thinking about? What pictures are coming into your mind? [The coach brings this new feeling into the branch of Thought.]

Client: I see how their lives could be. [The client's physiology shifts, his body relaxes, and he smiles.]

Coach: Although you can't be absolutely certain right now that those investors will share your vision of how you can transform the world, you can be certain that you can share your vision with them. What happens when you fly toward that? [The coach combines a belief from the Rules branch—that the client *can* share his vision—with the value of transforming the world from the Energy branch, spreading the change higher up the client's Tree.]

Client: You know, I guess it's only a flight…

Obviously more work needs to be done here, but the principle is clear. By noticing when the client makes a shift in his Tree of Life, particularly a shift into a positive place, the coach can use the quantum Zeno effect to keep that positive shift in place. By focusing the client's attention on that new, positive aspect of the Tree, the client's unconscious mind will have the opportunity to transform the rest of his Tree of Life in this new direction.

But before you can transform his Tree of Life, you need to understand where your client is starting from, meaning what his Tree of Life is actually like right now. The Tree of Life Coaching model provides you with a diagnostic tool for his problem.

Discovering Your Client's Current Tree of Life

There are essentially two ways to reveal your client's Tree of Life. The first way is to systematically go through each of the points on the Tree and ask your client what he is experiencing with respect to each point.

The second way is to simply listen to your client, ask him to expand on his problem, and notice what his conversation says about his Tree of Life. This takes a little more experience; you have to be very familiar with the branches of the Tree of Life in order to map your client's experience as he speaks in a conversational way. However, it can be much faster to find the problem branch because the client is likely to go straight there when associated into his problem.

Whichever of these two approaches you use, I strongly advise that you gather only enough information about the problem Tree of Life to allow you to help your client make some of the changes he wants. If you try to discover his entire problem Tree of Life, you may drop him so deeply in the problem that you will have difficulty bringing him out again and finding resources! On the other hand, if you make one small change to his Tree of Life, it may change everything. And you can always go back and revisit that Tree of Life later on to find more aspects that should be changed.

In the example below, I will show you how to use a more structured set of questions to discover your client's Tree of Life in the problem context. (For this example, I'll use a female client.) The conversational approach is similar but less structured. As you gain more experience in the formal process, you can move to a more conversational style, knowing you can return to the more formal analysis if necessary.

As usual, we'll start at the bottom of the Tree of Life. This method is based upon John Overdurf's coaching pattern from HNLP.

Opening question: What do you want to work through?

This question sets the scene and allows the client to raise her issue. Notice that I say "work through" rather than "work on" because this terminology begins to presuppose success, meaning that she will work through the problem to the solution on the other side.

We don't know exactly what a client's response will be to this question or where she will start exploring her Tree of Life. Will she tell you about the Real World context in which the problem takes place? Will she tell you about her thoughts or her feelings? Will she tell you what beliefs she holds about herself? Perhaps she will even tell you about the childhood incident that causes her to have the problem now.

Dr. Richard Bandler, the cofounder of NLP, often suggests a general rule that the very first thing the client says is the key to the solution to that problem. This is excellent advice. How does it fit in with the Tree of Life?

Within the Tree of Life Coaching model, we assume that the client knows unconsciously which branch of her Tree of Life is damaged or misaligned. So, for example, if your client says something like, "I can't see myself doing that," she is telling you that she literally cannot make the required picture within her mind. A mental image is a type of thought, so we are going to be working on the Tree of Life branch of Thought. On the other hand, if your client makes a gesture toward her body while saying something like, "I feel stuck…," she is telling you that the problem lies in the branch of Emotion or Energy, meaning feelings inside the body.

How You'll Be Able to Recognize the Problem Branch

Problems in the Real World

As I mentioned earlier, people do not come to see you for coaching because of problems in the Real World unless you offer skills-based coaching. The Real World is what it is. Instead, they come to see you because of a problem in their Tree of Life.

Problems in the Sensory Model of the World

You will know that the problem exists in a client's Sensory Model of the World when she says something like:

- "He makes me feel [negative emotion]…"
- "I do that [negative behavior] because…"
- "I can't do that [desired behavior] because…"
- "I'm not motivated [or some other feeling she can't access] when…"

These cause-and-effect types of sentences, where something in the Real World causes the client to feel a certain way or do a certain thing, or stops her from feeling a certain way or doing a certain thing, are constructed in her Sensory Model of the World. If you can change her Sensory Model of the World, you may well resolve her problem very quickly and easily.

Problems with Thoughts

If her problem lies in the branch of Thoughts, this means that she is making negative pictures inside her head or saying nasty things to herself, or that she can't make a certain type of picture about herself succeeding in her goals (which might program her unconscious mind for success).

If you are trained in NLP, you can also listen out for submodalities. Submodalities are the "qualities" of these types of internal representations (pictures, sounds, and self-talk), such as the size or location of an internal movie picture. So the client might say something like, "I can't seem to get any distance on the issue…" meaning that her internal picture is just too close. Submodality shifts can very quickly shift this kind of issue.

Problems in the Branch of Emotion

It's quite common, when your client has a problem primarily in the branch of Emotion (she is feeling a negative emotion such as fear, or she can't feel a positive emotion such as motivation), that her "left-hand" column (Thoughts, Rules, and Archetypes) will be blocked. If this is the case, she might say something like, "I don't know, I just feel…" She might well gesture to her body as she says this, indicating that the feeling is somatic (i.e., in her body).

A quick and easy way to address this sort of issue is simply to change the experience she has of the feeling inside her body. The simplest way of doing this is to ask her to stand up and shake the feeling off. This will change her physiology and therefore change her somatic feelings.

You could also use techniques such as Richard Bandler's "backward spin" technique by asking her to bring the feeling outside her body, changing it by reversing the spin, and then bringing it back inside her body.

Problems in the Branch of the True Unconscious

If the problem is primarily in the True Unconscious rather than another branch of the client's Tree of Life, she may very well be confused about the true nature of the problem and about why she does whatever it is that she does. Therefore, she may say something like, "I don't know why I do this…" but in this case the behavior itself won't necessarily be accompanied by a negative emotion, other than perhaps confusion, and may even be accompanied by a positive emotion.

It may be that the True Unconscious is picking up some information from Rules, Energy, Archetypes, or some other branch and using it to decide on the meaning of the context. Having defined the meaning, the client (or perhaps it is clearer to say the client's body, controlled by her unconscious) engages in the behavior.

These can be tricky problems to address directly because the client literally doesn't know. You can use so-called "process instruction" to reprogram the unconscious directly. Process instruction is a trance process in which the hypnotist essentially directs the client's unconscious mind to make any and all changes that are necessary to change the situation and the client's behavior.

Alternatively, you can dissociate her from the behavior, which in turn dissociates her from that problem Tree of Life. Hopefully she finds herself in a more resourceful Tree of Life, with a more positive rule book and positive values. You, as the coach, can then leverage this positive rule book and positive values to make her unwilling to return to the original Tree of Life.

To give a quick example of this "dissociation" pattern, suppose you have a client (a man, for this example) who has a problem with gambling. He doesn't really know why he does it, but he does know it's damaging his family because of the financial cost and also because of spending his time gambling rather than being with his wife and children. If you try to explore his gambling Tree of Life, he might find it very difficult to access and even more difficult to change. So an easier approach might be to find a different Tree of Life from which he can view the situation. You might, for example, ask him to associate into one of his children and view the situation from that perspective—from the Tree of Life of his child. You might ask him the following questions:

"Imagine floating into your daughter and seeing the situation from her perspective. Imagine being at her first softball game, with all her friends and their fathers…"

[This will root his daughter's Tree of Life in a specific context.]

"Imagine floating into your daughter and looking out of her eyes as you look around for your daddy… and you realize he's not there… What does that mean to you?… How does it make you feel?… What do you thinking about that, when you imagine where your daddy is?"

[Here we explore the lower triad of the daughter's Tree of Life…]

"You see that everybody else's daddy is there. Why do you think they came to the softball game?… So your daddy really should be there as well, shouldn't he?"

[Exploring the branch of Rules]

"What is important to you about wanting your daddy to be at the game? What do you think is so important to your daddy that he can't be there?"

[Exploring the branch of Energy]

"If you could have your daddy any way you wanted, how would he be?"

[Installing a new archetype]

"And if he was that way, what would be important to him about his relationship with you?... Would he have come to your softball game then? Why? How would he feel if he missed the game? How would he feel if he came to a game and watched you score a run? He'd be proud of you, wouldn't he?"

[Flowing the energy down from that new archetype in order to create a new Tree of Life]

"Now let's invite you to float out of your daughter and into the daddy that she wants to have—the daddy she would feel proud of, the daddy who would not let anything stop him from seeing her softball game, the daddy who would feel joy watching her play, who would be proud of her, as he watched her score that run..."

[Integrating the client's daughter's Tree of Life with the new and improved daddy Tree of Life, and associating your client into the new daddy Tree of Life]

Problems in the Branch of Rules

You'll know your client has a problem in the branch of Rules because he'll say things like "I can't," "I have to," "I should," and so on. In NLP, these are referred to as modal operators. Modal operators describe the rules that push us in one direction, pull us in another direction, and stop us from moving in a third direction.

Because we are now pretty high up in the Tree of Life, this is a place of high abstraction. Therefore, these Rules may be somewhat divorced from the Real World. For example, your client might say, "I wish I were more patient [meaning he believes he *should* be patient]." If so, it will be necessary to first root the Tree of life in the Real World by asking something like, "Tell me about the last time and place that you wished you'd had more patience…". The client's answer, "It was yesterday, I was playing with my kids…" provides a Real World context in which the Tree can be rooted.

Having rooted the Tree of Life in the Real World, you can then decide what to do about that specific Rule.

If the Rule is a good Rule in that context: In this case, you should ask for another context where the Rule is a problem: "It seems like that makes sense in that context. Can you tell me about another time when it was actually a problem for you?"

If the Rule is a good Rule in other contexts, but not in the context the client chose: This requires a "context reframe," keeping this Tree of Life for the other context and building a new Tree of Life in this context, perhaps starting with the branch of Archetypes. You might ask, "It seems that would be appropriate if you were in context Y, for example, but not in the situation you described. How would you like to be different there?"

A bad Rule in every imaginable context: Note that this is very rare—every feeling and every behavior has a positive intention, after all. It's much more likely that you, as the coach, could identify another context where the Rule would indeed make sense.

Problems in the Branch of Energy

Problems in the branch of Energy are likely to manifest themselves as problems in relation to the client's values or as either too much negative energy ("I always feel bluh…") or a lack of positive energy ("I can't find the motivation to…").

Once again, this is a fairly abstract branch of the Tree of Life, and you should make sure it is grounded in the Real World by asking for a specific context in which the problem arose.

A complete discussion of coaching around values is outside the scope of this book. However, you, as the coach, will know there is perhaps a problem in the client's values when he either does something he doesn't want to do (self-sabotage) or fails to do something he wants to do (lack of motivation).

In any case, when doing Tree of Life Coaching with a client, it is always a good idea to elicit and "clean up" his values. To learn how to do an effective values elicitation and cleanup, you might want to take an NLP Master Practitioner course. I will outline the typical steps here:

Step 1: Elicit the client's values in the specific context. Remember, always root the Tree of Life in the Real World.

Step 2: Rank the values elicited in step 1. Remove any duplicated values. You will likely end up with a short list of values, typically between three and seven.

Step 3: Make sure the values elicited are self-supportive by asking, "Does [lower value] support [higher value]? Does [higher value] include [lower value], meaning if you have [higher value], do you automatically have [lower value]?"

Step 4: Identify any "away from" values, meaning values about what the client does not want. You can identify these values by asking, "What does [value] do for you?" You are listening for anything that sounds like a negative, such as, "I value my family because I don't want them to leave me…"

Step 5: "Clean up" the client's values by making sure all the top values are "toward" values and that the number one value includes all the other values and is supported by all the other values. You can use the NLP technique the Visual Squash as one method to do this (see *The Visual Squash* by Jess Marion and Shawn Carson, in our NLP Mastery Series, for details).

If the client's problem is more around a level of energy that is not appropriate in that context—either a lack of energy in a context that requires the client to take energetic action, or too much energy in a context that requires more care and self-control—then you, as the coach, might want to explore with the client whether he is always this way or only this way in that specific context.

If he is only that way in that specific context, you might want to do a "context reframe," meaning to take the Tree of Life that contains that inappropriate energy and apply it to different contexts where it is more appropriate, and find a new Tree of Life for the context in which your client wants to be different. For example, if your client gets aggressive in business meetings, you might want to reapply the Tree of Life that includes the aggression to the sport's field and help your client find or generate a new Tree of Life for the business context that includes a more appropriate type and level of energy.

On the other hand, if your client demonstrates the inappropriate energy in many or most contexts of his life, you, as the coach, may need to teach him how to experience other, more resourceful, types of energy. Your client may need to experience these other types of energy often enough and in enough contexts that they become available to him whenever he needs them.

Problems in the Branch of Archetypes

You'll know that your client has a problem in the branch of Archetypes when he refers to some childhood event that causes the problem he is experiencing now or limits what he can be now.

Alternatively, he may say something like, "I've always been this way—I'm just like my mother." Either way, he's taking events from a past experience and modeling himself on those events.

You, as the coach, can address problems in the branch of Archetypes either by changing the archetypes he has access to (using "reimprinting," for example) or by providing him with a brand-new archetype, for example, using Deep Trance Identification.

Problems in Wisdom

Problems in Wisdom will tend to lead to recurring problems or perhaps a lack of "creativity." This is because your client is "always doing what he's always done and always getting what he always got." By creativity, I don't necessarily mean someone with writer's block. It could be someone who's stuck in a job or career, a relationship, or any other situation he doesn't enjoy, but who can't find a way to step out of that into something new. In fact, you can think of a problem in Wisdom as an inability to grow a new Tree of Life!

There is a risk for the coach in this type of problem. As coaches, we may feel the need to try to find a solution *for* the client. This may be just what he DOESN'T need when he has a problem in Wisdom (a difficulty in finding a new way forward). This is because if you give him a solution, he was not the one who found it, you were! So the next time he gets stuck in his new Tree of Life, he'll have the same problem: he'll still be stuck. You have given him a fish; however, you have not taught him how to fish!

As a coach, you might want to consider a way to give your client the tools, the methodology, to find a new way forward by himself. If you can do this, the next time he gets stuck, he won't need your help, because he will be able to find the solution by himself.

Problems in the Source

Problems in the Source can lead to a lack of trust that the universe is unfolding as it should. In a coaching context, this is sometimes referred to as a lack of resiliency. Resiliency allows you to respond to changing events around you so that if something unexpected takes place, you're able to deal with it.

Rest assured, the universe will always have something unexpected up its sleeve. Your client will have to face something that may throw him off his game. And as a coach, so will you! The key to resiliency is to understand that each potential Tree of Life is appropriate only for one specific context. When life gives you lemons, you need to make lemonade, and in order to make lemonade, you need the Tree of Life of a lemonade maker!

Step-by-Step Approach

Okay, so now you've asked your opening question,

"What do you want to work through?"

The client has answered you and given you the pearl of wisdom that would allow you to dissolve his problem in an instant. And you missed it! What do you do now? I will show you how to methodically lead your client to ascend his Tree of Life branch by branch in order to find the answer. You will begin by asking him questions about the Real World to ensure that you are working with a solidly rooted Tree.

Questions About the Real World:

First of all, you will want to root your client's Tree firmly in the Real World by finding out exactly where and when he has the problem:

"Tell me about the last time and place this happened... Where are you? What are you seeing? What are you hearing? What is happening?"

This leads your client to describe his Real World experience. By asking about what he is "seeing" and "hearing," you turn this into a sensory experience, and you associate the client into the context by using the present progressive tense ("seeing" rather than "see")

Questions about the Sensory Model of the World:

Okay, so now you have his Tree of Life rooted in the Real World. The next step is to discover the key element in his Sensory Model of the World. In order to do this, you have to find the exact point in time when something in the Real World "causes" him to do something he doesn't want to do or stops him from doing something he does want to do, or makes him feel something he doesn't want to feel, or stops him from feeling something he does want to feel. In HNLP, John Overdurf calls this process "stalking the wild synesthesia"!

You, too, can stalk the wild synesthesia by associating your client into the Real World situation as described above and then asking him to tell you "what is happening" (again, note the present progressive tense, which will keep him associated as he tells you the story). At some point, you will see his state change as he goes into his problem. In order to find the precise moments he goes into the problem, you might have to rewind and play his memory tape a few times: "What happens just before? What happens next?"

By asking about what happens just before an event or just after an event, you can gradually move the action forward and backward through time. Once again, what you're looking for is the exact point at which the client loses control of his state. You'll know he's lost control of his state because you'll see a physiological shift—probably a change in facial expression and a change in posture. When you see the shift, you can ask: "What just happened? What are you seeing right now? What are you hearing right now?"

You are seeking to discover the "trigger" that causes your client to lose control. The trigger will be something in the Real World. For example, if he has a fear of public speaking, the trigger is likely to be seeing the eyes of the audience upon him or imagining seeing the eyes of the audience upon him. You have now discovered his Sensory Model of the World, which includes something like:

- The audience looking at me *means* they are judging me.

- Being judged *makes me* feel nervous.

Going Further

Okay, so now you have discovered the Real World context in which your client's problem Tree of Life is planted, and you have discovered his map of the world that makes his problem possible. You have now discovered the first two branches of his Tree. Congratulations!

In fact, you now have all the information you need to begin to resolve his problem. You see, all you have to do now is to plant a new Tree of Life within that Real World context. This new Tree of Life will replace the old Tree of Life, and your client's experience will be transformed.

Of course, you're likely to want to explore that problem Tree of Life a little more so you have all the pieces you will need in order to work elegantly within Tree of Life Coaching.

Questions About Thoughts:

"What are you seeing right now? Where is that picture? How big is it? Is it framed or unframed? What are you saying to yourself?"

These questions will uncover what and how your client is thinking. They will also tell you something about the "submodalities" he is using. Submodalities are all of the finer distinctions within our thoughts. For example, if I am thinking in pictures, the size of the picture is a submodality.

When you have planted, and nurtured, a new Tree of Life for this context, it will probably mean that both the content of your client's thoughts and the submodalities of his thoughts will be changed.

Questions About Feelings:

Please be aware that you should not ask your client a lot of questions about his feelings when he is in a negative state because these

80

questions will make him feel worse. In addition, these questions are generally unnecessary unless you are going to be working directly on a feeling, for example, using the "backward spin" of NLP, or EFT, or a similar modality. If you are working directly on the feelings, you can ask questions such as:

"Where do you feel that? Does it have a size and shape? Which way is it moving? What color is it?"

If you're not going to be working directly on the feeling, all you have to do is explore the Real World context until you see him physiologically shift into his problem state. This tells you all you need to know.

Questions About His Rules and the Beliefs He Holds in This Situation:

"What are you believing about yourself? What are you believing about the world around you?"

Please be aware that, in general, if you can make the change at the lower levels of the Tree of Life, you won't necessarily need to find out about his beliefs in the problem state unless you ask when you first associate him into the problem. This is because if you lead him into a positive state (either in the branch of Emotion or in the branch of Energy), and attach that positive state to the Real World trigger (the trigger that previously triggered the problem), then that belief may automatically change as that Tree of Life reorganizes itself.

However, if you're finding it difficult to make a change to the branch of Thought and Feelings, the client may have a limiting belief that is preventing him from changing. So, for example, if you are doing a new strategy installation from NLP (a sequence of experiences in the lower triad of the Tree of Life) and it doesn't seem to be working, you might want to shift up to the Level of Rules to make the change.

There are many patterns of belief change that you could use, such as the various NLP belief change patterns, but I will discuss that later in the book.

Questions About His Values:

"What's important to you about that? What's important to you about being different in this situation? What's important to you about making this change?"

Again, it's generally easier to make changes at the levels of thoughts and feelings. However, if you're not able to lead him to the change he desires, he may be blocked by an inappropriate value or by conflicting values. If you have to change his values, you can use the values elicitation and cleanup discussed above.

Questions About His Active Archetypes:

"Where did you learn that? Who taught that to you?"

This may reveal an archetypal experience from childhood that you could change using reimprinting.

Higher Branches of the Tree of Life

If you're working in the higher branches of the Tree of Life—Wisdom and the Source—or the branch of Archetypes if you are installing a new archetype, you may not be so concerned about your client's current Tree of Life. This is because changing these higher levels will often lead to a complete transformation of the entire Tree of Life.

Chapter 6: Using the Tree of Life to Create an Awesome Coaching or Hypnosis Protocol of Your Own

In this chapter, I will show you how my colleagues and my stop smoking protocol uses the principles of "destructive deduction" and "creative induction" to begin to take apart the client's smoking Tree of Life, to generate a new smoke-free Tree of Life, and to move around the Tree of Life and set this new Tree in place in all the major branches. I will also show you how our protocol begins to move energy between the various branches to link them up, how it begins to put tension on the new Tree of Life in order to test its resiliency, and finally how the protocol firmly roots the new Tree of Life in the client's Real World.

It's worth saying a little bit about destructive deduction and creative induction—terms coined by the great strategic thinker John Boyd—before I move on to discussing the smoking protocol. Destructive deduction, within Tree of Life Coaching, refers to focusing on one of the branches of a problem Tree of Life and chopping it off using some coaching, hypnosis, or other change-work pattern. Creative induction refers to the process of installing one positive branch and allowing a new Tree of Life to grow from that branch; it's rather like taking a cutting from a healthy tree and using that cutting to grow an entirely new tree.

If you take a look at our stop smoking protocol (which was largely developed by my colleague Jess Marion; you can find it described in detail in our book *QUIT: The Hypnotist's Handbook to Running Effective Stop Smoking Sessions,* by Jess Marion, Sarah Carson, and Shawn Carson), you'll find that we use the following techniques and patterns. (For this example, I will use the pronoun *she* throughout.)

1. Values elicitation involving asking the client why she wants to quit before she even comes to the session
2. Elicitation of end state energy (ESE) using the attention-shifting coaching (ASC) model from HNLP
3. Reframing to change the client's beliefs about smoking and quitting, and the client's Sensory Model of the World
4. "Craving busters" such as EFT or Richard Bandler's "backward spin" to change emotions and feelings within the client's body
5. Metaphors to offer the client new reference experiences
6. A "future self Deep Trance Identification" to begin to build the new smoke-free Tree of Life for the client
7. The "walk-through" pattern to embed an appropriately negative movie about cigarettes within the client's mind and to anchor it to appropriate negative emotion
8. The famous Perceptual Possibilities Pattern ("P-Cubed") to install an appropriate Sensory Model of the World and to anchor that model with appropriate representations (internal movies) and emotions
9. The Smoking Destroyer to delete and replace unhelpful memories about smoking
10. The Tiger Pattern to directly change the client's Real World behaviors by attaching the old smoking behavior to appropriate negative emotions and the anti-smoking behaviors to appropriate positive emotions
11. The Dreaming Arm Pattern to allow the client's unconscious mind to create and select new, empowering behaviors

12. Direct suggestion within deep trance to reinforce all aspects of the smoke-free Tree of Life that is being installed
13. The Swish pattern from NLP to attach, or root, the new smoke-free Tree of Life to all the contexts in which it will be needed (i.e., all the contexts in which the client used to smoke)
14. The HNLP Testing Loop to test the resiliency of the new Tree of Life and thereby make it stronger
15. The Final Ritual to root the new smoke-free Tree of Life in the here and now

If this seems like a lot of patterns, it is, and they all add to the success of the protocol. Let's take a look at the protocol as a journey around the Tree of Life.

When a client first calls to book a session to quit smoking, we ask her why she wants to quit now. We're listening for the answer to link to some of the client's values. As you know, values lie on the branch of the Tree of Life called Energy. If the client does not have a personal, internally framed reason for wanting to quit, for example, if she says, "…because my husband/doctor told me I should," we will typically not take her on as a client. If she wants to quit because her doctor tells her she should, this reason lies on the branch of the Tree of Life we call Rules. In our experience, a Rule telling her that she "shouldn't smoke" typically won't give her enough energy to change her Tree of Life unless it is also accompanied by her own internal value.

Of course, she may know many good reasons for wanting to quit, but these reasons may not carry a lot of energy for her personally. This might be the case if she's found these reasons by reading information on the Internet but has not connected *emotionally* with those reasons. In this case, the energy is flowing from what she knows—the branch of Thoughts—to the branch of Energy, and it's very hard to maintain this upward flow within the Tree of Life.

In order to help her find a source of energy that can flow down the Tree of Life, we like to use Attention Shifting Coaching (developed by John Overdurf) to move her into Wisdom. Attention Shifting

Coaching uses creative induction to lead the client into a state of confusion. For example, we might ask, "What's everything else about being smoke-free that you haven't yet considered?... And what's important to you about that?" A full discussion of Attention Shifting Coaching is beyond the scope of this book, but essentially you are leading the client into a place where her unconscious mind can find reasons to quit, based upon values that resonate with her.

Having identified these values, we have begun to move down the Tree of Life from the branch of Energy, first visiting the branch of Rules, using reframing to change any inappropriate beliefs about said personal ability to quit smoking and any other inappropriate rules that may hinder her quitting.

Next we move down to the branch of Emotion, showing her how she can use techniques such as EFT or the "backward spin" from NLP to change her emotional state in the moment from craving (for example) to something much more positive. We then root this in the Real World by suggesting that she can use these techniques whenever she needs to if she feels a craving or if she has a negative emotion that would have previously led her to smoke.

You will notice that up until now, we have been making changes to undermine her existing Tree of Life—the smoking Tree of Life. We are now going to return her to the top of the Tree and begin to construct a brand-new smoke-free Tree of Life. We begin by returning to the branch of Archetypes. We might share some metaphors around smoking and quitting. These metaphors provide the client with reference experiences, which lie within the branch of Archetypes.

Staying in the branch of Archetypes, we now invite the client to step into her "future self," meaning how she will be when she is a healthy non-smoker. Having an experience of this new identity, we will invite her to construct a new Tree of Life by asking her questions such as:

- Where are you when you are this way?
- What are you thinking, as you're there?

- How are you feeling, now?
- What are you believing about yourself, now?
- What's really important to you, now?
- Look back and notice the memories you have after an hour of being a healthy non-smoker…

Notice that although we are inviting her to associate into her *future* self, as soon as she does so, we switch into the present tense so that it becomes her *present* self. This questioning allows her to construct the new smoke-free Tree of Life. Of course, the state is still a little fragile—more of a sapling than a fully grown Tree!

At this stage, we're going to leave this new smoke-free Tree of Life to begin to grow by itself. As it does so, we are going to return to the old smoking Tree of Life and chop it down. After all, it's less a Tree of Life than a tree of death! We aggressively hack at each of the branches in turn. There is no particular order to this, and we will cycle through this "deductive destruction" as many times as necessary to get the job done.

We lead the client through the "walk-through" pattern in order to destroy any positive pictures (i.e., thoughts) she may have about cigarettes and smoking. Instead, we install a negative internal movie of the cigarettes and smoking (i.e., a Thought) and also attach it to the appropriate negative Emotions.

We use the P-Cubed Pattern to install an appropriate Sensory Model of the World, where smoking *causes* health issues and other negative outcomes, while making a decision to quit and being smoke-free *causes* a long, healthy life and other positive outcomes. This model is also reinforced using the appropriate negative and positive emotions.

We use the Smoking Destroyer to destroy any positive archetypal memories the client may have of smoking and replace them with appropriate negative memories of smoking and positive memories of her own sense of control. We do this by recalling the memory of that first cigarette and changing it using the neuroscientific concept of "reconsolidation" (i.e., reimprinting).

We use the Tiger Pattern to cause energy to flow between the actual physical behaviors of smoking—in particular, the client raising the cigarette to her lips—in the Real World and appropriate emotions in the branch of Emotion. We do this using classical conditioning to attach the act of smoking to negative emotions and the act of not smoking to positive emotions.

At this point, that old smoking Tree of Life lies in ruins. We have chopped it down using destructive deduction. Meanwhile, the smoke-free sapling of life has been taking root and growing in the background. We now turn our attention to this new Tree of Life and nurture it using the following techniques.

We use the Dreaming Arm to allow the True Unconscious to work with the creative Void to create and select new Real World behaviors that she can use instead of the old smoking behavior. The Dreaming Arm uses the principles of the NLP six-step reframe to do this.

We use direct suggestion within deep trance to reinforce all the aspects of the new smoke-free Tree of Life.

We use the NLP Swish pattern to move energy around the branches of the lower triad of the new smoke-free Tree of Life. We do this using internal representations (pictures) of how she wants to be smoke-free, and attaching these pictures to the positive emotions that these pictures generate. We then attach these pictures to the "triggers" in her map of the world (represented by people, places, or objects in the Real World). As a result of this pattern, each time she sees a trigger that might previously have led her to smoke, it now generates a thought-picture of how she wants to be a non-smoker, together with positive emotions that being a non-smoker bring.

At this stage of the process, that old smoking tree of death as been destroyed, and the new healthy smoke-free Tree of Life is growing strongly in its place. We start to test and strengthen this new Tree of Life through testing. For example, we ask her to consider how she feels now in each of the contexts in which she used to smoke. This questioning strengthens the roots of this new smoke-free Tree of Life in each of those contexts.

Finally, we use a ritual in which the client is asked to throw away her last pack of cigarettes to root this new smoke-free Tree of Life in the here and now.

Hopefully, the above explanation shows how our stop smoking protocol uses the principle of destructive deduction to destroy the client's old tree of death, and the principle of creative induction to replace it with a new, healthy, smoke-free Tree of Life. This simply requires cycling through the various branches of the old Tree of Life and moving energy between branches of the new Tree of Life.

Using the Tree of Life to Construct Your Own Protocol

You can use the above model to construct a protocol for any client issue. If you're trained in a discipline like NLP, you probably have many tools to change each of the branches.

But even if you're not trained in a discipline that offers you a number of different tools, you can use the simplest of tools to change any particular branch. Suppose you want to do something like "Simple EFT" (SEFT, or tapping). The EFT technique often focuses on the branch of Emotion, using a script something like, "Even though I have this [emotion], I still deeply and completely love and accept myself… This [emotion]… I choose to let this [emotion] go… I choose to feel [positive emotion] instead…"

You can easily redirect EFT to your client's Real World behaviors, to triggers in her Sensory Model of the World, to her thoughts, to her beliefs and other Rules, to her values, to memories and other Archetypes, simply by replacing the word *emotion* with something else. So rather than simply tapping on the negative emotion, you can follow that up by tapping on other negative aspects of your client's current Tree of Life:

- "…the thought of…"
- "… my belief that…"
- "…my desire for…"
- "…my memory of…"

And so on. You can then begin to grow a new positive Tree of Life by tapping on:

- "I choose to feel…"
- "I choose to imagine…"
- "I choose to believe…"
- "I choose to value…"
- "I am gifting resources to my younger self in that memory…"
- "I choose to do…"

So you can modify even the simplest technique to be applied to any and all branches within the Tree of Life. You can also start energy flowing around the Tree of Life by linking one branch with another:

- "As I think about my new feeling, I believe…"
- "These new feelings mean…"

And so on. I will expand on this idea in the next chapter.

Exercise

1. Think about an issue that many of your clients come to see you for.
2. Consider what the Tree of Life of your typical clients who have this issue is like.
3. Consider what a more appropriate Tree of Life might be like for these clients.
4. Develop a protocol that moves from the first Tree to the second Tree, changing or even destroying the first Tree using

the principle of destructive deduction, and creating and nurturing the second Tree using the principle of creative induction.

Consider the following questions:

- Where should I start changing the first Tree? Which branch?
- Should I move up the first Tree from there, down the first Tree, or in some other direction?
- At what point should I leave the first Tree to create the second Tree?
- What branch should I begin with in creating the second Tree? In which direction should I move then? (Hint: The easiest way to create a new Tree of Life is starting in Archetypes and flowing the energy downward.)
- How will I move between the first Tree and the second Tree? For example, will I seek to totally destroy the first Tree before moving to the second Tree? Or should I simply destabilize the first Tree, plant the second Tree, and then return to the first Tree to complete its destruction? Or should I leave most of the first Tree in place and simply prune one or two branches?
- How should I root the second Tree in the client's Real World?

Once you have built your own protocol, you need to begin to test it out. You can test it on your clients if you have an active coaching practice, or you can join a coaching or NLP practice group, for example on MeetUp. Remember, your Tree of Life protocol is an organic process; it will change as you test it and learn what does and doesn't work. Do not be afraid to discard things that don't work and add new things to test!

Chapter 7: Incorporating the Tree of Life into Your Coaching Modality Using the Lightning Path

In this chapter, I will show you how to incorporate the Tree of Life into your current coaching modality, if you happen to use a more prescriptive system. By "prescriptive system," I mean one that might not offer the flexibility to allow you, as the coach, to lead your client freely around the Tree of Life. For example, you might use hypnotic scripts in hypnosis or a very formalized and "scripted" method of EFT or EMDR, and so on. The common thread that we will be working with is any system of change work that teaches you to apply pretty much the same prescribed sequence of steps no matter who your client is and no matter what his or her issue is.

To do this, I will borrow one of the principal tools for using the Tree of Life from the Kabbalah—the "Lightning Path." The Lightning Path allows you to ascend the Tree of Life from the Real World to the Source and then return down the Tree of Life, branch by branch, back to the Real World. This may sound a little complex, but it's really quite simple.

The Spiritual Meaning of the Lightning Path

One can say that mastery of the Tree of Life has been achieved when you can rise up the Tree of Life to return to the Source and then bring that learning and that energy back to the Real World. In spiritual terms, you can think of this as becoming enlightened, but rather than leaving the world and going to Nirvana as a Buddha, you choose to stay on Earth as a Bodhisattva, or enlightened being, who remains on Earth to become a teacher of others.

Although there are many pathways you could use to ascend the Tree of Life, the Lightning Path is the most common traditional path. The Lightning Path travels from the Real World to the Source, passing through each of the branches on the way. The route of the Lightning Path is:

- From the Real World
- to the Sensory Model of the World
- to the branch of Thoughts
- to the branch of Emotions
- through the True Unconscious
- to the branch of Rules
- to the branch of Energy
- to the branch of Archetypes (this may be as far as you need to go within the coaching context)
- to Wisdom
- and finally to the Source

The Lightning Path then returns from the Source to the Real World, following the same path:

- From the Source
- to Wisdom
- to the branch of Archetypes
- to the branch of Energy
- to the branch of Rules
- through the True Unconscious
- to the branch of Emotions
- to the branch of Thoughts
- to the Sensory Model of the World
- and finally back to the Real World

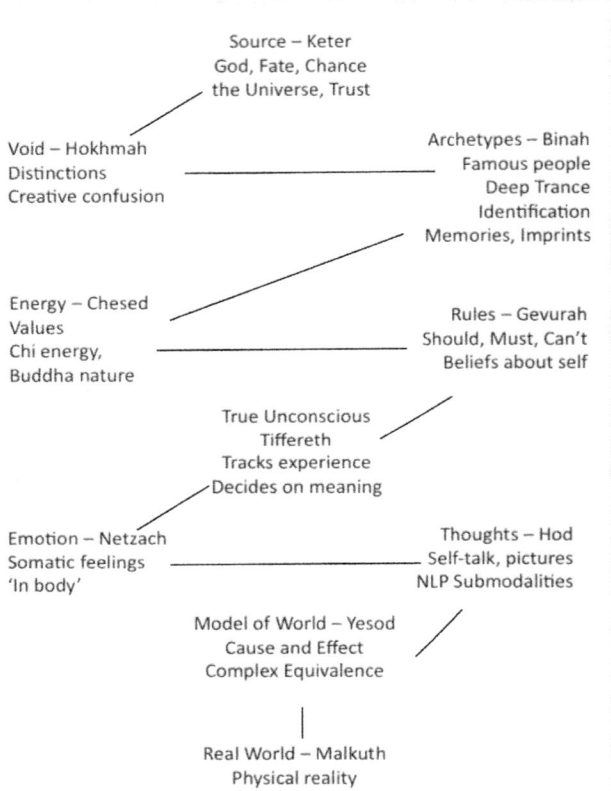

Incorporating the Lightning Path into Your Coaching

It is very easy to incorporate the Lightning Path into your current coaching modality. All you have to do is to ask the client to focus on each of the branches in turn on the way up and on the way down.

On the way up to the top of the Tree of Life, your aim will be to loosen (in the worst case), or transform (in the best case), the client's current problem in each of the branches.

On the return journey down the Tree of Life, your aim will be to install and strengthen a new, totally transformed Tree of Life. As you return to the Real World, you will root this new Tree of Life in the context in which your client is seeking change.

Using the Tree of Life in this way allows you to transform your client's problem into its own solution, no matter how the problem is structured. This is because it allows you, as the coach, to tackle the problem from a number of different perspectives and angles.

Using the Tree of Life in Practice

So how would this look in practice? The details will depend upon the coaching or change-work modality you use. So on the surface, it will be very different if you're doing EFT, or if you're doing classical hypnosis with direct suggestion, or if you're doing EMDR, and so on. But on a deeper level, the sequence would be the same, so let's take a look at that.

Step 1: The Real World

At the start of the session, ask your client (a man, for this example) where he wants a change in his life. As usual, be as specific as possible so that you can root the change work in one specific time and place. It's much easier to generalize after you've helped him change this first event than it is to try to change a number of events at the same time.

Step 2: Move Up to His Sensory Model of the World

Ask him what is taking place in this specific time and place. Make sure he is associated and speaking in the present tense so that you can explore the actual Tree of Life in that context, not what he thinks the Tree of Life might be. As the coach, you'll be looking out for the "cause" of his problem. What is it exactly that makes him feel like behaving the way he doesn't want to?

Now, take this as his problem. You can now use your chosen modality to begin to loosen this branch of the Tree of Life. So, for example, if your client tells you that his boss "makes him feel bad" (a cause-effect from his Sensory Model of the World), and suppose you are using EFT as your change-work modality, you might tap on something like:

"Even though my boss is an a**h***, I deeply and completely love and accept myself" (or whatever EFT script you use).

Step 3: Move On to the Branch of Thought

When you have helped your client loosen his old Sensory Model of the World—the one that's causing him a problem—you can move up to the branch of Thought. It's important to note that by making a change in the Sensory Model of the World, you will likely have also made a change in the branch of Thought. Therefore, you should not assume that he will be thinking about the original problem; you should simply ask him what he is thinking in this context, now.

Bear in mind that when we're working in the branch of Thought, it is not simply about what the client is *saying* to himself; it is also the pictures he is making inside his mind. So you might ask him, "What are you thinking? What pictures are you making inside your mind?"

Whatever he tells you his problem thought is, take this to be his problem, his presenting issue. Now apply your technique to his problem thought.

Staying with the EFT example, suppose your client tells you that he imagines his boss looking at him and frowning, and that makes him (your client) feel anxious. So at least one of the thoughts your client is having is a picture-thought of his boss frowning at him.

You can now lead your client to tap on, "My boss frowning at me…," or you could use the EFT movie technique on the movie of his boss frowning at him.

Step 4: Move Over to the Branch of Emotion

Once again, it's important to realize that the changes you made to your client's Sensory Model of the World, and his thoughts, may well have led to changes in the branch of Emotion. You shouldn't necessarily expect your client to be feeling emotions consistent with his original problem; the emotions may have changed. You should simply ask him for that feeling now, when he imagines being in the context.

Whatever he tells you, unless it's positive because of the changes you've already made, becomes the presenting issue on which you work. You can then apply your modality or techniques to this new presenting issue.

You can then lead your client to loosen or transform that emotion using your chosen modality. Staying with EFT, you might tap on, "Even though I'm feeling this anxiety, I deeply and completely love and accept myself... This anxiety..."

Step 5: Move Up Through the True Unconscious to the Branch of Rules

Hopefully you're getting the hang of this by now. Ask your client questions about the branch of Rules. These questions might include: "What you believing about yourself? What are you believing about the world? What do you have to do in this context? What should you do in this context? What are your options in this context—what can you do?"

Again, bear in mind that he may say things inconsistent with the original problem because of the changes you have already helped him make.

Take whatever he says that's negative as the new presenting issue. Use your chosen modality to begin to loosen it or transform it.

If he is now holding positive beliefs, you can reinforce these by telling him how well he's doing!

Step 6: Move Across to the Branch of Energy

Ask your client what is important to him in this context, now, meaning his values. Alternatively, ask him who he will be as a person when this is no longer an issue for him. Or if you feel he's already made a major shift, ask him who he is now that he has made this change.

Once again, he may have changed, by changing the original problem. Starting from where your client is NOW, use your chosen modality to loosen any negatives and reinforce any positives.

Step 7: Move Up to the Branch of Archetypes

You can now lead your client up to the branch of Archetypes.

Ask him to imagine his future self who has not only made this change but who is so far beyond the problem that he can't even imagine having it. Then ask who he is as a person when he looks back from this future time and sees how far the change has generalized to other areas of his life.

If you, as the coach, feel that he's already substantially transformed the problem as you moved up the Tree of Life, you can associate him into this future self. "Imagine stepping into that future you..." If you feel that he is not ready for this yet, you can simply ask him to imagine seeing his future self in front of him.

Whether or not you choose to associate your client into his future self, you can use your modality to reinforce the changes he has made so far.

Once again using the example of EFT, you might lead your client to tap on something like: "I choose to step forward into this future me!"

Moving up to the branch of Archetypes may be sufficient for most coaching purposes, unless you're involved in very spiritual coaching. So now you will begin to move back down the Tree of Life.

Step 8: Move Down to the Branch of Energy

Ask your client what is important to his future self. If he is fully associated into his future self, you should see a big shift in his physiology.

Even if he is seeing his future self in front of him, you're likely to see his physiology shift somewhat. If you do see a good physiological shift, you might want to associate him into that future self at this point.

Once again, you can use your chosen modality to reinforce this change. For example, if you're using EFT and he tells you that his future self values freedom, you could tap on: "I choose to be free."

Step 9: Move Over to the Branch of Rules

Ask your client what his future self is believing. Once again, the response will vary depending upon whether or not he is associated into his future self at this stage. Use your chosen modality to reinforce these new positive beliefs, perhaps with something like:

"I have the power to choose…"

Step 10: Move Down to the Branch of Emotion

Because Emotion represents feelings inside the body, it's necessary for your client to be associated into his future self in order to truly experience the Emotion branch of that future self. If you haven't already associated your client into his future self, now is the time to do so.

Once your client is associated into his future self, ask him what he is feeling inside his body. Use your chosen modality to increase the intensity of these positive emotions.

Step 11: Move Across to the Branch of Thought, Then Down into His Map of the World, and Finally into the Real World

As we are now reapproaching the Real World, it is time to begin reassociating with a Real World context.

As your client is feeling the positive emotions he found in the last step, ask him to think about the trigger and notice how it's different. This step will trigger new thoughts in his mind, and these thoughts will imply a new map of the world as he sees(imagines) the Real World trigger that used to give him the problem.

You may wish to ask your client to imagine stepping into the old context with this new feeling and noticing what he sees, what he hears, and how he is behaving. Essentially, you are asking him to future pace the new Tree of Life. If there is any inconsistency or return to the old problem Tree of Life, you have to move him back up the Tree of Life because you may have missed something the first time. Remember, Tree of Life Coaching is an organic process. Sometimes it takes several iterations of this pattern to reach the final positive Tree of Life.

Conclusion

Using the Tree of Life in this simple way allows you to add a great deal of flexibility, even if you're working in a change-work modality that is otherwise quite prescriptive. Remember, all you have to do is to visit each branch of the problem Tree of Life, ask the client about it, and treat his response as the presenting issue for your modality.

On the flip side, if you are working in a more client-centered modality, the Lightning Path provides a road map for the coaching process that ensures that you, as the coach, are able to address all aspects of the problem while helping your client become more of who he wants to be on a profound level.

Chapter 8: The Tree of Life Coaching System

In the previous chapter, I explained how you could take the Tree of Life model and incorporate it into your current coaching style, whether that style is client-centric, is based on the use of different protocols for different problems, or focuses on one "scripted" modality.

In this chapter, I will be talking about how you can use the Tree of Life as one integrated coaching system. I'll show you some specific tools that you can use to shift issues in each of the branches of the Tree of Life. I will also show you how to focus your coaching efforts on one part of the Tree of Life or another, depending upon the effect that you want to get. Alternatively, you can cycle through the various branches and areas of the Tree of Life in multiple sessions to generate more profound change in your client, an approach I will discuss later in this chapter.

In Chapter 9, I will show you how to coach in the lower triad of the Tree of Life—the branches of Emotion, Thought, Sensory Model of the World, rooted in the Real World. This type of coaching is particularly useful for clients who simply wish to gain more control over their peak states.

In Chapter 10, I will show you how to coach on the right column of the Tree of Life—the branches of Wisdom, Energy, and Emotion (again, rooted in the Real World). This is particularly useful for clients who come to see you for an issue that involves feeling something they don't want to feel—perhaps a fear of speaking in public—or not feeling something they do want to feel, such as motivation.

In Chapter 11, I will show you how to coach on the middle triad of the Tree of Life, in particular the branches of Energy, Rules, and the True Unconscious. The True Unconscious is particularly important as the central crossroads of the whole Tree of Life.

In Chapter 12, I will show you how to coach on the right column of the Tree of Life—the branches of Archetypes, Rules, and Thoughts, rooted as always in the Real World. Coaching on the right column is particularly useful for clients who get in their own way through their own negative thoughts and beliefs. I'll also talk separately about coaching in the branch of Archetypes as part of the Upper Triad in Chapter 13 because of the importance of this branch in being able to generate an entirely new Tree of Life.

Finally, in Chapter 13, I'll talk about the Upper Triad of the Tree of Life, the Source, where the energy enters the Tree and flows down to creative Wisdom and manifests in archetypes.

Protocol for Tree of Life Coaching

You, as the coach, can focus on any one of the areas or regions of the Tree of Life, or indeed on any individual branch, to help a client resolve an issue or become more of the person he or she wishes to be. However, if you're in a more long-term coaching relationship with your client, you might want to focus your coaching systematically through the Tree of Life. In this section, I will provide one way in which you can do this. Please don't take this as the only way, and feel free to modify it based on your own preferences or the particular needs of your client.

Step 1: The Real World

In any coaching situation, I urge you to ask your client for a specific context in which he or she wants to be different. As I have stressed many times in the course of this book, a "specific context" means one specific time and place in the past, in the future, or right now. Clients very often want to change everything at the same time, but this spreads their energy over many contexts rather than focusing all their energy on one, making any change more difficult to achieve.

In contrast, when you focus on one specific context, it becomes very easy to change that one time and place. It becomes much easier to release any negative emotions from that one specific context and step into a peak state in that context. Once your client has been able to change one specific context, the next change, in a similar context, becomes that much easier. And the change in a third similar context becomes simple. And then your client will find that every other similar context is changed as well. The human brain is a great generalization machine!

I suggest that you start each and every one of the steps that follow by revisiting your client's Real World context for change. (For the following steps, I'll use a female client as the example.)

Step 2: The Lower Triad (see Chapter 9)

It's a great idea to make sure that your client begins by having control over her physiology, her senses, her thoughts (i.e., her working memory), and her emotional state. Teaching this control to your client through coaching in the lower triad will make the rest of the coaching process much easier.

Starting with Thought and Emotion will give you and your client control over her peak state. This is vital for effective change work because change always and only takes place in the present moment as the human brain rewires itself; being able to step into a peak state and attach that state to any context is the ultimate driver of change.

Once she has control over her Emotions and Thoughts, she can fully open up her sensory filters to take in more information from the world around her.

It's also great for her to begin to understand that her personal Sensory Model of the World does not faithfully correspond to reality itself and that her personal interpretations are coloring, and creating, her experience. Once your client understands this, she can choose which filters she applies to test specific models of the world for usefulness, discarding those that don't work and keeping those that do.

Step 3: The Right-Hand Column (see Chapter 10)

Once your client is in control of her Emotions, Thought, and Sensory Model of the World, you can turn to dealing with specific issues she may be facing. Very often these issues arise simply from being in an inappropriate state in a specific context. For example, your client may feel stressed at work, or fearful in front of an audience, or out of control in the presence of alcohol or drugs, or whatever her specific problem is.

Coaching on the right-hand column provides you, as the coach, the opportunity to rewire your client's neurology to attach more useful and positive emotional states to those contexts. For example, you might attach focus to the work context, confidence to the audience, or self-control to the bar.

It is important to remember that even when coaching in the right-hand column, you may need to lead your client back to the branch of Thought (for example, to handle any negative self-talk) or to the branch of Rules (for example, if your client has a limiting belief that interferes with the change).

Step 4: The Middle Triad (see Chapter 11)

The client is now in control of her moment-to-moment experience, through lower triad coaching, and also has access to appropriate positive emotional resources in the difficult contexts in her life. It is now time to give her some direction by coaching in the middle triad.

Coaching in the middle triad will allow her to realign the values that drive her behaviors. Values that drive people's behavior—their unconscious values—are very often much different from the values they claim to have when asked—their conscious values. This realignment will make the client's unconscious values and her conscious values agree and will align her behavior with these values.

Coaching in the middle triad will allow her to transform limiting beliefs into empowering beliefs. These empowering beliefs will act as a positive book of rules for living her life.

Finally, by exploring her values and beliefs, your client can come to understand how the True Unconscious mind draws on these in making meaning in her life.

Step 5: Coaching the Left-Hand Column (see Chapter 12)

You will have already shown your client how to control her immediate thoughts (Thoughts) in coaching the lower triad, and you will have shown her ways of changing her beliefs (Rules) in coaching the middle triad. Now, coaching the left-hand column should be fairly straightforward. As the coach, you can review the branch of Thought and the branch of Rules; however, the major work will be done in the branch of Archetypes.

When coaching on the left-hand column, you should pay particular attention to your client's memories, especially memories that provide her with inappropriate reference experiences. For example, if your client has performance anxiety about speaking in public, she may have recent memories about embarrassing situations when she had to speak in public or memories from childhood about being told that she should be "seen but not heard" or told that her ideas did not have value. These experiences should be transformed using the neuroscience concept of "reconsolidation" (changing memories by bringing in new emotional resources) into more empowering experiences.

Step 6: Visiting the Source and Using Wisdom to Install Resiliency (see Chapters 15 and 25) and Using Archetypes to Generate an Entirely New Tree of Life

The Source represents the energy of the power of creation entering the universe, or entering your life, or your client's life. If you're religious or spiritual, you may think of the Source as being God, or if you wish, you can simply think of the Source as being chance, or the hand of fate. There will come a time in your client's life when something unexpected happens. This may be an opportunity, for example, for her to relocate to another state or even another country to pursue a dream career, or it could be a tragedy that totally changes your client's life. Either way, your client needs a way to cope with the unexpected by taking advantage of opportunities and adapting to necessities.

When coaching the right-hand column, we visited Wisdom in order to unconsciously identify resources that the client could use in specific contexts. But Wisdom also offers the opportunity to develop resiliency. Why do I say this? Because Wisdom provides the opportunity to develop a new way of looking at the world when chance, fate, or the hand of God changes everything. Remember, Wisdom starts with no preconceptions, no Model of the World, no distinctions between good and bad, right or wrong—simply the oneness of the universe at that point in time. Visiting Wisdom allows your client to take that raw experience and "split" it into distinctions, good or bad, useful or not useful, opportunity or threat. These distinctions may be very different from the ones that your client held before visiting Wisdom.

The branch of Archetypes can be used to take the creative energy of the Source and Wisdom, and turn this energy into actionable values, beliefs, emotions, thoughts, a new Sensory Model of the World, and actual behaviors. This process involves installing powerful new Archetypes for your client based upon the principles of Deep Trance Identification.

Step 7: Trees within Trees

Tree of Life Coaching is an organic process. When you plant an acorn and grow an oak tree, that is not the end of the process—it's just the beginning. That tree produces new acorns, and those acorns fall to the ground, where most of them disintegrate back into the soil. But one or two germinate into new saplings at some point, and the original oak tree itself will die, providing nutrients for the trees to come. In the same way, your client's Tree of Life has to have the flexibility to adapt and even to be cut down and replaced by something better.

Just as the acorns need to fall to the ground in order to find out which of them will become a new oak tree, your client has to return her attention to the Real World to identify what is not working in her current Tree of Life. To do this, she should be looking for the exceptions, the differences. As human beings, we have a tendency to look for events that confirm our worldview, a psychological process known as "expectancy bias." But it is the exceptions that reveal the limitations of our current worldview and our current Tree of Life.

Each exception I observe offers me an opportunity to prune and improve my current Tree of Life, and even to plant a new sapling that may grow into something amazing.

As a coach, you need to install in your client this flexibility, this willingness to let go of the old and replace it with the new.

Chapter 9: Coaching in the Lower Triad

Coaching in the Lower Triad can be enormously effective. Indeed, many popular methods of coaching stay almost entirely within the lower triad. By the lower triad, I mean your client's Sensory Model of the World, his or her thoughts, and his or her feelings or emotions (in the Kabbalah, this is sometimes referred to as the world of Yetsirah). To this, we are going to add the Real World; after all, there is no point in controlling your thoughts and emotions or building a new map of reality unless it is applied, and has a positive effect, in the Real World.

Because these four points combine to produce our complete experience at any specific moment in time, you can very often help your client make all the changes he or she wants only using these four points. After all, if your client ends up being in charge of his or her own emotions, thoughts, and behaviors, your client will probably be pretty happy!

There are a number of modalities that work within this lower triad. The most obvious example is something like body massage, which operates in the Real World and aims to reduce the level of physical tension within the physical body. When the muscles and joints of the body are relaxed, it typically leads to a mental and emotional relaxation in thoughts and emotions.

Other modalities operate within the lower triad by moving around from point to point. A good example is cognitive and behavioral therapy (CBT). CBT typically aims to identify specific contexts within the Real World that generate negative feelings in the client (i.e., in Emotion). CBT then asks the client to move across from Emotion to Thought and use Thought to begin to make the desired change. So the client is encouraged to identify the "thoughts" leading to the negative emotions—thoughts such as imagining the very worst that could happen ("catastrophizing"). The client is encouraged to think *about* these thoughts (applying Thought to Thought) and to consider whether they are really likely to happen in the Real World context. If they are, the client can take preventive or corrective action, but if they are not likely (as is usually the case), thinking about the "catastrophizing" thought in this way can lead to a reduction in the negative emotion. And because these "catastrophizing" thoughts arise from the client's Sensory Model of the World, when enough of them are challenged, the client's Sensory Model of the World also changes in a feedback loop. And when the client's Sensory Model of the World changes, his or her reaction to the Real World changes, and his or her thoughts and emotions change.

Of course, this is somewhat of an oversimplification of the points of the Tree of Life that are involved in CBT. After all, CBT is also ultimately likely to wander into the area of belief, not just thought. However, typically the originating point of CBT is to challenge the thoughts that the client has at a specific moment in time.

In the rest of this chapter, I am going to give you an overview of a coaching method that my colleagues and I developed to coach within this lower triad. The pattern has four pieces or steps, each step broadly corresponding to one of the points within this lower triad (plus the Real World).

The method is called the BEAT Coaching System. If you want to learn more about the BEAT, you can read our book, *The BEAT Coaching System*, by Shawn Carson and Sarah Carson, available at Amazon.com.

Overview of the BEAT System

The BEAT system follows four steps, each represented by one of the letters of the word BEAT. My colleagues and I always teach the steps in the order B-E-A-T, partly to fit in with the acronym BEAT but also because this is typically the easiest order in which to do the steps. However, there is no reason you can't do the steps in a different order within the Tree of Life Coaching model, depending upon what you feel your client needs.

The four steps are as follows:

- B: Check in with your physical body, especially your physiology, your posture, and your breathing. Your physical body exists within the Real World, of course.
- E: Check in with the emotions you're feeling in your body. If you discover that they are negative, this step gives you the opportunity to change them.
- A: Check in with your awareness, what you're paying attention to, and how you're paying attention to it. This step broadly corresponds to the Sensory Model of the World; I will explain later why this is.
- T: Check in with your thoughts. Once again, if you find that your thoughts are negative, this step gives you the opportunity to change them.

To do the BEAT in real time, simply move your attention around each point of the pattern, first your body and breathing, then your emotions, then your sensory awareness, then your thoughts. The BEAT System is based on the belief that if your body, your breathing, your emotions, your sensory experience of the world around you, and your thoughts are all aligned with how you want to be, you will generally be performing at, or close to, your best.

You can try the BEAT right now if you wish:

B: Body and Breath

Notice the position of your body. If you're curled up on the sofa reading this book, you might want to stand up to make it a little easier.

- Are your feet relaxed and balanced on the floor, with your weight equally distributed over the surface of each foot and between your feet? Or is your weight carried on your heels or your toes, or shifted over to one leg or the other? The result of not distributing your weight evenly between your feet is that your hips move out of alignment, of course.
- Is your spine elongated and straight, with your head floating on top as if suspended from the sky? Or are you stooped over or leaning to one side or the other?
- Are your shoulders and arms relaxed? Or are you carrying tension in your shoulders, arms, and hands?
- Is your breathing deep and even from the within your belly, or is it shallow and from your chest?

Your body instinctively knows how to feel relaxed. So as you check in with your body and breathing, make any adjustments that you need to make to feel relaxed. If your body is not balanced over your feet, if your spine is not straight and balanced, or if you carry excess tension in your body, this can cause long-term health problems.

E: Emotions

The second step of the BEAT is to notice your internal emotional state. This means that you go inside your body and check how you're feeling. It's important that you don't check inside your *mind* to discover how you're feeling—you check inside your *body*!

If your emotional state is good, there's nothing further to be done. However, if your emotional state is in some way negative, you now have the opportunity to change it.

A great way to change your emotional state is to use your thoughts through visualization to reverse the "spin" of your emotions. You can do this with the following steps (taken from the "backward spin," developed by Dr. Richard Bandler, cofounder of NLP):

- Notice where in your body you feel the emotion.
- Notice in which direction the emotion begins to move first.
- Notice the path by which your emotion returns to its starting point.
- By following this path, notice in which direction your emotion is "spinning."
- Once you have located the path in which your emotion moves from its starting point and returns to its starting point, imagine taking that pathway outside your body; literally see your emotion spinning in front of you.
- Now reverse the direction of the spin so that it's moving in the opposite direction.
- Now bring this new emotion, spinning in the opposite direction, back inside your body and notice how it's different.
- If you wish, you can add a favorite color into the new emotional spin or add sparkles, or laughter, or anything else you choose to make it feel better now.

A: Awareness – Sensory Model of the World

The next step of the BEAT is to check in with your sensory attention. This is not just what you're paying attention to, but also *how* you're paying attention. You see, you have two types of attention, which I call foveal attention and peripheral attention. These are terms that are generally applied to your eyes—your vision—but the same principles apply to all your senses.

Foveal attention is what your conscious mind generally pays attention to. The fovea of your eye is the central part that is designed to see detail. For example, as you are reading this book, you're moving your eyes so that the fovea of each eye is able to read each word in turn. This is called foveal vision. If we apply this concept to your hearing, or auditory sense, "foveal hearing" is the sounds you are paying attention to. So, for example, if you are in a noisy bar talking to a friend, you will focus your "foveal hearing" on what your friend is saying.

In contrast, peripheral attention is all the other sensory information that your eyes and ears and nose and skin are taking in, but that you're not consciously aware of. So, for example, if you are reading a book in the park and somebody throws a ball toward your head, you are likely to automatically duck to avoid it because your unconscious mind is tracking everything else in your visual field. This peripheral vision takes place in the outer portion of the retina of the eye, which is designed to see movement. Similarly, when you're in that noisy bar speaking to your friend and you hear your name mentioned in a conversation across the room, your ears might prick up because your unconscious mind was paying attention to all the background sound.

How does this relate to the Tree of Life? Well, in many ways your sensory attention arises from your Sensory Model of the World. The things that you choose to pay attention to, and how you pay attention to them, reflect what is important and what you consider to be cause and effect within your Sensory Model of the World. Why is this? Because your model the world *determines* what you pay attention to and how you pay attention. If, for example, your Sensory Model of the World suggests that your boss *makes* you feel bad, you are likely to either pay close attention to your boss or alternatively try to avoid paying any attention at all to your boss by paying attention to everything that is not-your-boss. Either way, your Sensory Model of the World determines your attention.

Let's consider another example. Within your client's Sensory Model of the World, speaking in front of an audience is a threat to her because her audience is judging her. This is likely to result in her attention being on the eyes of the audience, the gateway to judgment. This is what you will likely find when you work with people who have performance anxiety when they have to speak in front of a crowd— they become fixated on the eyes of the audience and either notice those eyes or purposefully look away so they don't have to notice the eyes of the audience at all.

Let's move on and consider how we can pay attention to the world in a resourceful way. Note that I am not telling you *what* to pay attention to, but *how* to pay this attention. One way of paying attention to the world that can be very useful and powerful is to begin to pay conscious attention to your peripheral senses. This is the opposite of our normal way of paying attention, which is for your conscious mind to pay attention only to your foveal vision.

The easiest way to describe this is using the visual sense. If you want to experience it, just try this simple exercise. Read all the instructions before you begin, or ask a partner to read the exercise to you and follow along as he or she reads.

- Hold your hands in front of you at shoulder height (as if you are sleepwalking).
- Now turn your hands vertically so your fingers are pointing to the ceiling or sky and you can see the backs of your hands (as if you are pushing a door open).
- Look between your hands at a point on the wall in front of you, or something in the distance if you are outside. Keep your eyes on that for the rest of the exercise.
- Begin to wriggle your fingers. Notice that you can see your fingers moving even though your focus is on the wall beyond them.
- Now begin to move your hands apart (as if you are opening a curtain), but keep wriggling your fingers. Notice that you can still see your fingers moving even though your focus remains on the wall in front of you.
- Move your hands all the way out to the side and notice the point where your fingers seem to disappear and you can no longer see them moving. This point is the very edge of your peripheral vision.
- Bring your hands just a little bit back so you can see your fingers moving again. Keeping your gaze on the wall in front

115

of you, realize that you can see every object around you, above you, and below you. You're now in the state that I call peripheral vision, or the coaching state.

The coaching state is a very powerful state to be in—not just for the coaching but for many other activities as well. Peripheral vision allows you to be consciously aware of things you would otherwise miss, such as unconscious movements that your client makes.

T: Thoughts

The final piece of the BEAT System is to begin to pay attention to your own thoughts and to begin to control the contents of your thoughts.

The easiest way to do this is through a mechanism in your brain called "working memory." Working memory is a system, or a network of systems, that are designed to transmit information between your conscious and unconscious minds. Working memory consists of three elements:

- A visuospatial sketchpad (essentially a movie screen) that shows pictures or movies. It also allows you to mentally manipulate complex visual symbols.
- An audio loop (essentially, a soundtrack to the movie).
- A title to the movie (essentially, what the movie means to you).

So when you're in a specific context—say, a meeting at work—the thoughts that you can generate by using your working memory might be:

- A movie of how you want the meeting to go and how things will look when you have achieved your goal
- An appropriate and inspirational soundtrack to the movie
- An appropriate, positively stated, and inspirational title to the movie

So, for example, if you're in a sales meeting and you want your prospects to sign an agreement, you might imagine a short movie of them smiling at you, shaking your hand, and signing the agreement, with a soundtrack of them saying, "Thank you for bringing me this opportunity!" The title of the movie might be *Making the Sale*, or *Helping the Client*, or something more inspirational and abstract, perhaps *Doing What I Was Born to Do!* or even *Ka-ching!*—whatever works for you!

Keeping positive, outcome-based movies in your working memory tells your unconscious mind what you want to achieve.

Using the BEAT within Tree of Life Coaching

If you have a client come to see you for a very specific change and that problem does not seem to be based upon negative beliefs about him- or herself, or misaligned values, or a lack of a powerful self-identity, or other more abstract elements that you might find higher up the Tree of Life, it may be sufficient to focus on the lower triad of the Tree of Life. The BEAT System is a great way of doing this.

Of course, the BEAT System by itself does have its limitations. For example, the BEAT does not help you know what you should be doing, because it doesn't tap into your values, which are located in the branch of Energy. But it does help you be your best in the moment, and that by itself is a pretty good start to achieving your dreams!

Most of the clients who come to me for coaching have not spent a lot of time thinking about their own beliefs, or their values, or the archetypes that express themselves in their life. They may be strongly in touch with one or two memories, particularly if those memories are negative, but they haven't fully considered the role that memory plays in their current experience, choices, and behaviors. For this kind of client, the BEAT is a great place to begin the coaching relationship because it is so real and so tangible.

Once you have taught your clients the BEAT as a way to step into an ideal state, they have a tool that they can use anywhere, at any time, in any context. It truly is a wonderful tool. And if you begin coaching a client on a long-term basis, using values coaching, for example, you can add the other points of the Tree of Life to the great foundation built on the BEAT System.

Chapter 10: Right Column Coaching

In this chapter, I'll talk about a specific type of coaching that focuses on the right column of the client's Tree of Life. The column begins in the Real World and then moves up through Emotions, Energy, and into Wisdom.

I refer to this as the "right column" because your client will tend to look to his right-hand side when processing information on this column. For example, he's likely to look down and to his right when he is processing emotions or other sensations within his body. He is likely to look up and to his right when he enters Wisdom. Of course, if you're facing your client, *his* right will be on your *left*. I will talk a little more about eye accessing for the right column later in the chapter.

I am going to use John Overdurf's coaching model, including his end state energy coaching and attention shifting coaching, as the main tools for right column coaching. However, I will also discuss more general "values-based" coaching models that focus on this part of the tree.

The philosophy behind this type of coaching is that you perform at your best when you have control over your emotional state. And when you are in a peak emotional state, everything else will tend to align with this, including your thoughts, your beliefs about yourself, and so on.

State-Based Performance

What do I mean by state-based performance? Let's take an example. Suppose you're making a presentation to showcase your company's services to a prospective client. Is the presentation likely to go better if you are feeling nervous or if you are feeling confident? Obviously, it's going to go better when you're feeling confident because that confidence is going to communicate itself to the client in how you stand, how you gesture, how you use your eyes, the tone of your voice, and a thousand other unconscious signals you send. So when you say, "My company has the resources to best meet your needs," you will sound confident about that. In contrast, if you're not feeling confident, you will be more likely to come across as being unsure about whether or not your service is actually a good fit, and your prospect will pick that up either consciously or unconsciously.

But now let's assume that your prospect raises a question about whether or not your service is really a good fit for her. You could, of course, remain in your state of ultra-confidence and try to persuade your client that yes, indeed, your service is the best. However, it may be better to move into a state of curiosity, creating a space that will allow you to fully explore the prospect's concerns or thoughts that underlie that question. After all, if you don't know what her concerns are, you're not in a good place to address them. Once you have fully explored these concerns from a state of curiosity, it would be appropriate to move back into your state of confidence as you address each of the concerns in turn.

So this type of coaching is not just about teaching your client to go into a strong positive state. It's also about teaching your client how to move into an appropriate emotional state.

One way to think about this is that there is a set of key states that may be important in any human interaction. Exactly what these states are will differ depending on whom you might ask. For example, Edward de Bono, in his book *Six Thinking Hats*, describes six states, represented by six hats of different colors that are "worn" in turn in any decision making.

The six hats are as follows, together with their loose correspondence with the Tree of Life branch:

- White Hat: Facts and figures—representing Thought in the Tree of Life
- Red Hat: Emotions—representing Emotion in the Tree of Life
- Black Hat and Yellow Hat—representing negative and positive thoughts about any idea, what could go wrong, and the possible benefits. These represent extremes of the possible Sensory Model of the World from worst case to best case. These Hats also tend to pull in beliefs (from the branch of Rules) and values (from the branch of Energy).
- Green Hat: Creativity—representing Wisdom in the Tree of Life and also Archetypes, as de Bono suggests taking on other personalities
- Blue Hat: Control and decision making—representing the True Unconscious (combined with Thought)

The interesting thing is that de Bono suggests that we adopt a posture appropriate to each Hat (for example, adopting the posture of Rodin's *Thinker* for the White Hat), make an internal picture of the Hat (i.e., make a picture of the Hat in working memory), and so on. At the end of the day, what de Bono is suggesting is that we create a whole Tree of Life for each Hat. Six Thinking Hats translates to six different Trees of Life containing six different states and resulting in six different modes of thinking.

Ultimately, under right column coaching, what is really important is the ability to attach an appropriate strong positive emotional state to a specific context in the Real World. Which state is most appropriate is open to you, or your client, to decide. Confidence would be attached to one set of contexts, curiosity to another set of contexts, joy to another set of contexts, and so on.

We will now turn our attention to a way to create a state that is specifically tailored to your client, based on his or her needs within the context in which he or she wants to be different.

John Overdurf's Coaching Pattern, End State Energy, and Attention Shifting Coaching

John Overdurf's basic coaching pattern has the following steps, or questions that the coach can ask:

- What do you want to work through?
- Tell me about the last time and place this happened (the Real World context). Where are you? What are you seeing and hearing? What's happening?
- That's how you've been. How do you want to be different?
- And when you are feeling that (new emotion), where do you feel it in your body?
- And as you're feeling that (new resourceful emotion), look back at that Real World context and notice how it's different now...

This coaching pattern is structured in this specific way to lead the client (in this case, a man), and the client's brain, through a specific sequence of steps:

1. To associate him into the context of the problem so that the neural network associated with this context "lights up." Asking the client to describe the last specific time and place triggers this.
2. To dissociate him from the negative emotion he has previously felt in that context so the neural network associated with this negative emotion is temporarily "turned off." Pushing the problem into the client's past does this: "...that's how you've been...."
3. To identify and associate into a new positive emotion and to light up the neural network associated with this positive

122

emotion: "…how do you want to be different… where do you feel that in your body…."

4. When the network associated with the new positive emotion is lit, to simultaneously light up the network associated with the context: "…as you're feeling that… look back at [the context]…." Lighting up both neural networks at the same time begins to wire them together (neurons that fire together wire together – Hebb's Law).

Of course, it is not enough to just run through this pattern once and expect the resourceful neural network to be wired to the context in which the client wants to be different. The three keys to this pattern are repetition, repetition, and repetition!

You can find an in-depth discussion of this coaching pattern, including the underlying neuroscience, in *The Meta Pattern*, by Sarah Carson and Shawn Carson, available at Amazon.com.

So now the neural networks associated with the new positive emotion and the Real World contexts have been wired together using Hebb's Law. Now, whenever the client is in that Real World context, the Tree of Life that will appear in that context will include that new positive emotion. The client will then be able to perform at his best in that Real World context. The pattern is simple and effective.

John Overdurf's End State Energy Pattern

John takes his coaching pattern to a higher level by incorporating the concept of "end state energy." You can think of end state energy as a resourceful emotional state that is also a value—what John calls an "enduring state of being."

Let's take a quick example. Suppose you have to give presentations to clients as part of your job. As I said above, it's going to be great if you can feel a sense of confidence as you walk into each presentation. But what sort of "confidence" do you want to have? For some people, confidence is a high-energy state of excitement; however, it can be exhausting to have to step into, and maintain, a high-energy state like that several times a day. Instead, you may choose to have a sense of confidence that is a little lower in energy but more enduring—something you can maintain all day. Rather than "high-energy excitement," it might be described as "calm certainty."

It is these lower-energy, but more enduring, states that we will be looking for when our coaching is focused on end state energy. End state energies may include states such as "freedom," "curiosity," and so on—states that are, or are closely related to, values.

When you, as the coach, lead your client into his end state energy, you provide him with a resource that can be available to him at any time. He doesn't have to expend a lot of energy to step into that state. So if you merely teach him how to feel confident by attaching that feeling of "high-energy excited confidence" to a particular context, that's wonderful. But your client has to generate a lot of internal energy to step into that excitement. Consider a high-energy speaker such as Tony Robbins. He is reputed to keep a small trampoline in his backstage area so he can bounce up and down and build up the amazing energy he shows onstage. Unfortunately, we don't all have access to trampolines when we need them!

On the other hand, if you teach your client how to be "confident" by generating a lower-energy but more enduring state of "calm certainty," that can always be available to him. You don't need to bounce on a trampoline to be confident—you just need to know how be calmly-certain!

Because we can hold these lower energy states and values for our entire lives, they reside in the branch of the Tree of Life that I call Energy, the point directly above Emotion. The branch of Energy represents the emotional energy we are born with or that we have developed over a long period of time.

And because the branch of Energy is in the Tree of Life above the branch of Emotion, there is a flow of energy from the Energy branch down to the branch of Emotion. Therefore, by tapping into your client's end state energy, he can feel positive emotions within his own body.

You can encourage your client to find this type of end state energy by directing his unconscious attention toward this higher-level nature of this energy. You can do this by subtly changing the questions you ask. In the example of the coaching pattern given above, I asked the question:

- "That's how you've been. How do you want to be different?"

Sometimes I might even ask, "How do you want to feel different?" In any case, many clients will believe that this is what you actually asked them, even though you actually asked them about their identity ("How do you want to be?"), not their feelings ("How do you want to feel?").

So, if your client has been feeling anxious, he might reply, "I want to feel confident!" Very often a client chooses a high-energy emotional state that is the "opposite" of the high-energy negative emotion he or she has been feeling.

You can make your question more explicitly about end state energy by asking the question as:

- "How do you want to be, as a person, different from how you have been?"

Asking the question in this way makes it clear that you're not necessarily asking him about how he wants to feel in the moment, but rather about how he wants to be as a person over the longer term. This question is more likely to lead to the client finding an end state energy than a more immediate (high-energy) emotion.

Of course, once your client has found his end state energy, you can easily turn it into a more high-energy emotion simply by asking him where he feels it in his body. Remember, energy tends to flow downward through the pathways of the Tree of Life. Having a more high-energy emotion that arises out of an end state energy makes the whole coaching process go much faster and more easily because it is the high-energy positive emotional state that create endorphins in the brain—neurochemicals that help cement Hebb's Law and wire the positive emotional state with the context faster.

Consider the following example (this time with a female client):

Coach: What do you want to work through?

CLent: I get anxious when I have to give a presentation.

Coach: Tell me about the last time and place you felt that way... [rooting her Tree of Life in the Real World]

Client: It was on Tuesday...

Coach: Where are you? What are you seeing and hearing? What's happening?

Client: I'm in the office, I'm giving a presentation to a customer, my boss is sitting in, and I see her starting to frown as I speak...

[The client's face drops, she begin to slump, and the tone of her voice changes. This lets you, as the coach, know that the client has accessed the negative emotion, which, of course, she keeps in the branch of Emotion.]

Coach: Well, that's how you been. How do you want to be as a person that's different from how you've been?

[You, as the coach, use shifts in her physiology and voice tone in order to dissociate the client from the negative state and give her the space to find a resource.]

Client: I want to be free to be myself. [This sounds like an end state energy, in the branch of Energy.]

Coach: What's it like when you're feeling free... being yourself...? Where do you feel that in your body? [The coach seeks to have the end state energy "free" move down into the branch of Emotion, meaning a sensation in the body.]

Client: It's great... I feel it in my heart!

[The client's face lights up, showing the coach that the client is accessing the resource of "being free" in the branch of Emotion.]

Coach: And as you're feeling that now, make it even bigger! [The client's shoulders straighten....] That's right! Take a look at your boss's face and your customer's face and notice how it's different now!

You'll notice from the above example that what the coach does is to lead the client into an end state energy (freedom) and then turn that end state energy into a much higher energy emotional state, which the coach then attaches to the context by asking the client to "take a look at your boss's face."

In terms of Tree of Life Coaching, the coach has:

- Explored the client's current Tree of Life by associating the client into the Real World context and checking on her emotional state in Emotions (which the coach sees in the client's physiological responses)
- Led the client to step out of that Tree of Life by dissociating her from the context
- Led the client to step into a new Tree of Life at the higher level of Energy. This new Tree of Life contains "freedom" at the Energy branch.
- Led the client's energy to flow down from the branch of Energy into the branch of Emotion by asking the client where she feels the freedom in her body. Remember that the

127

Emotion branch contains feelings that we feel inside the body. The coach also helps the client build up the level of energy within the new positive emotion.

- The coach then attaches this new positive emotion to the Real World context by asking the client to see her boss's face and her customer's face. Remember, these were the elements of the Real World context that had previously led the client to feel the negative emotion, i.e., the trigger.

Attention Shifting Coaching and Entering Wisdom

When your client is skilled at handling different emotions—both negative emotions and positive emotions—it may be sufficient to work in the branch of Emotion on the Tree of Life. When working with this sort of client, he or she will easily be able to step out of negative states and access positive states.

If your client doesn't have complete control over high-energy resource states such as excited confidence or outrageous joy, you may want to work in the branch of Energy because it may be easier for your client to tap into end state energies. Remember, end state energies are typically lower energy but more enduring.

Sometimes you will have a client who finds it difficult to access either positive emotions or positive end state energies. This is very often because the client is either "stuck" in one or more negative states or because he or she is more "intellectual" and not very in touch with his or her feelings. These clients may find it easier to access positive end state energies, and positive emotions, by first entering Wisdom.

Remember, Wisdom is often associated with a state of mild confusion. It's a state of confusion because it's also a state of wholeness—a place where it's no longer necessary to make distinctions between "this" and "that," between one thing and another. In Wisdom, there is no longer certainty because everything is (or is connected to) everything else.

There are many ways of entering Wisdom. If you want to experience Wisdom for yourself, a fun, easy way is to find or draw a picture of a Necker Cube. A Necker Cube is a drawing of a wireframe cube or box. It's possible to see the Necker Cube as a three-dimensional cube in one of two orientations. Take a moment to look at the picture and find one of the orientations. Once you can clearly see the first one, shift your gaze until you can find the second one.

As you look at the picture, you can hold one of these orientations in your mind for a few seconds. Now switch your perspective and see the cube from a different direction for a few seconds. Now switch back to the first orientation. Now switch to the second orientation. Allow your mind to switch back and forth between the two orientations, holding each one in mind just long enough for it to be firmly fixed before switching to the other.

As you go through this exercise, you may find something beginning to shift in your mind—a sort of flexibility that develops as your brain tries to hold two conflicting ideas at the same time. This is a great exercise for creativity: simply think for a few moments about the problem you're working on, then look at the Necker Cube and go through the above exercise for a few minutes. Then return the original problem and notice what's different about it.

If you want to go into Wisdom on a more permanent basis, you might want to study Zen Buddhism. For example, the koans of Zen Buddhism are mental puzzles designed to have no rational answer. Indeed, any attempt to answer the puzzles rationally is met with contempt and sometimes violence by the Zen teacher! For example, possibly the most famous koan asks, "What is the sound of one hand clapping?" It's easy to find rational answers to this question. For example, you could say "silence," or you could give no answer at all and allow your own silence to answer the question. But these types of answers miss the point of the question, which is to find an answer beyond rational "this" or "that."

Of course, you are wondering how you can lead your clients into Wisdom within a coaching context. One excellent way to do this is to use John Overdurf's attention shifting coaching. A complete discussion of attention shifting coaching is well outside the scope of this book. However, in brief, the system uses a sophisticated set of questions to first dissociate the client from where he or she is now, secondly to take the client into Wisdom, and thirdly to lead him or her to land in a resourceful landing spot in the Energy branch of a new Tree of Life.

The only way to really explain this is to give you an example. Suppose you have a male client who says, "I have performance anxiety. I'm afraid of speaking in public."

First of all, you're going to want to take the client out of his anxiety and fear. One way to do this is to use "spatial" language to physically shift his unconscious mind away from that anxiety and fear. So you might say something like:

• "Aside from that anxiety…"

This may sound like a throwaway phrase that doesn't have a lot of meaning, and that's certainly true as far as the conscious mind is concerned. But from the point of view of the unconscious mind, it's very different. For the unconscious mind, *aside* is a word known as a "spatial preposition," meaning a word that tells you where something is. *Aside* literally means "to the side of." It therefore implies that the client is no longer "inside." By saying "aside from," you are telling the unconscious mind to step out of the anxiety and fear, and to move to one side.

Next you're going to want to move your client into Wisdom. A good way of doing this is to use "inductive" language, meaning language that asks the client to consider everything at once.

To take a silly example, suppose I have a female client who is afraid of purple penguins, and I ask, "Aside from penguins, what's everything else in the world that is not purple?" Or to be more extreme, "What's everything that is any color other than purple?" Or to be even more extreme, "What's nothing that's any color other than purple?" Even though grammatically these questions sound as if they make sense, the part of your brain that deals with putting objects into categories simply gets overwhelmed with the magnitude of the ambiguities within the question. The result is a moment of confusion. And that is Wisdom.

So to incorporate the second step, you might ask the client with performance anxiety:

- "Aside from that anxiety, what's everything else you haven't been paying attention to...?"

You have already asked the client's unconscious mind to step out of the anxiety, and now you've added a piece that will tend to lead him into Wisdom.

However, simply confusing people is, at best, a little hit and miss; the client might gain some insight when the confusion passes, but he might simply go back to where he was. So to make this process more directed, you might add a suggestion that he find a value. Remember, values are generally positive and are kept in the Energy point on the Tree of Life. Values, lying in the branch of Energy, can easily be used to generate powerful positive emotions because energy tends to flow down the Tree of Life.

To do this, you might add to the question:

- "What's truly important to you?"

This asks his unconscious mind to find a value—something that's "truly important" to him. So the question becomes:

- "Aside from that anxiety, what's everything else you haven't been paying attention to that's truly important to you?"

131

Finally, you want to root this new Tree of Life (or perhaps it's better to say this new sapling of life) within the Real World. You can do this by adding the word *now* to the question. *Now* brings the client's unconscious attention to the here and now, which is a Real World context.

So putting these four pieces together, you might ask the client:

- "Aside from that anxiety, what's everything else you haven't been paying attention to that's truly important to you, now?"

This sounds like a very conversational question, but when delivered with a sense of intense-caring-curiosity (something that John Overdurf calls the coaching state and that Igor Ledichowski calls H+), this type of question can produce profound changes and insights for the client.

Putting It All Together

Let's put all the steps together in this example:

Coach: What do you want to work through?

Client: I have performance anxiety. I freak out every time I have to speak in public!

Coach: Tell me about the last time and place this happened... [The coach asks this question to ground the issue in the Real World by asking for the Real World context.]

Client: It was last week in the office.

Coach: What day was it? Where are you? What are you seeing? What you hearing? What's happening?

[The coach asks for more details about the Real World context to further ground the experience and to find the contextual triggers that

132

lie in the Sensory Model of the World. In practice, these questions would be asked sequentially rather than all at once, depending upon the client's responses.]

Client: It was on Tuesday. I was in the conference room giving a presentation to a customer. My boss, Michael, was sitting in on a meeting. I was explaining something to the client, and Michael starts to frown...

[The client's physiology begins to shift into a negative state as he enters the negative state in the branch of Emotion. This is sufficient exploration of the negative Tree of Life for now, so the coach shifts the client out of this Tree of Life using dissociation....]

Coach: That's how you've been. How do you want to be different?

[The coach invites the client to choose another emotional state that lies on another, more resourceful, Tree of Life. The coach first leads the client to the branch of Emotion.]

Client: I don't know—I just don't want to feel that anymore.

[The client is not able to step out of the unresourceful Tree of Life to find a new positive emotion.]

Coach: I understand. Let me ask you this: who will you be as a person when this is so far behind you that it is no longer an issue?

[The coach seeks to dissociate the client from the negative emotion of anxiety by taking him "forward in time." The coach also shifts the conversation to how the client wants to be "as a person," implying a more enduring state of being. This is more likely to be found in the branch of Energy on the Tree of Life.]

Client: I'm afraid I'll never put it behind me... [The client demonstrates that he is still speaking from his original Tree of Life, the one that contains fear and anxiety.]

133

Coach: I can understand why you don't see that yet, so let me ask you a question. It may sound a little odd, but I would like you to deeply and completely consider the question before you answer... Aside from that performance anxiety... what's everything else... you haven't been seeing... that will show you what's truly important to you... now...?

[The client gazes up and to his right. He looks slightly confused for a moment, which shows that he has entered Wisdom.]

Client: I don't know... [The client sighs, his body relaxes, and he laughs.]

Coach: What was that?

Client: I don't know—it just all seems so funny now...

[The client has come out of Wisdom and has landed in a good place. It may not seem obvious that humor was the answer to the problem, but the client's unconscious mind clearly thinks it is, and that's good enough!]

Coach: You seem like a person who appreciates a good joke. Where are you feeling that now in your body?

[The coach draws the value of "humor" down into a physical feeling in the body, moving from the branch of Energy down into the branch of Emotion in the client's new Tree of Life.]

Client: I feel it all over. It's sort of like a tingling or my skin... [The client is now feeling the value within his body, i.e., as an emotion.]

Coach: That's right—you feel it all over, like a tingling on your skin. [The coach repeats back the client's words to solidify the emotion.]

And as you're feeling that now, take a look at your boss's face and notice how it's different...

[The coach takes the humor-emotion that is being felt in the body and reconnects it with the Real World context, in this case, the client's boss's face.]

Making the Change Stick

Of course, a pattern such as the one shown above done once is unlikely to create a lasting change within the client. This is because to make the change permanent, we have to wire together the context—seeing the boss frown—and the new resource—feeling the humor. And we have to make this wiring permanent. To do this, we have to use repetition.

We also have to ensure that the rest of the client's Tree of Life is aligned with the change.

Coaching the Right Column and Eye Accessing

Eye accessing refers to a client's eyes moving as you move through the different steps of the coaching process. In the classic NLP model of eye accessing, emotions are typically accessed by looking down and to the right, while imagining new pictures, which we call "visual-create" in the NLP model, are typically accessed by looking up and to the right. Visual-create is associated with Wisdom because it represents seeing future potential—"the art of the impossible," if you will.

The description above is for some who is "normally organized," meaning the usual eye accessing cues. Some people might be organized differently or might even be completely reversed. We will stick with the classic NLP model for this discussion, but as a coach, it's important for you to calibrate your individual client's eye accessing cues.

When you are coaching, it can be useful to watch out for these eye accessing movements because they provide clues as to how the client is processing information. Of course, they only provide a part of the picture, and further clues are provided by the client's choice of words, physiology, and other behaviors.

When you are coaching on the right column of the Tree of Life, you might expect to see your client look down and to his right (if he is normally organized) when he associates into the context of his problem and begins to feel the negative emotion.

You will then want to help him move that negative emotion into his past using his own eye accessing cues. You can do this, for example, by taking hold of his negative emotion from the space down and to his left, with your right hand, and then move your right hand across your own body as if you're moving that emotion over to his left (meaning your right, assuming you are facing him).

This may sound complex, but just imagine you're grabbing something from his right hand and throwing it away to his left. As the eyes track the movements of your hand, the client's unconscious mind will put that negative emotion in the past.

To lead your client into Wisdom, you can raise your left hand, palm toward him, into his upper right visual field (which represents Wisdom). As the client's eyes track the movements of your left hand, he will look up and to his right and will tend to go into Wisdom. And when he emerges from Wisdom and finds his value for end state energy, he's likely to attach it to the palm of your hand (simply because that's what he's looking at).

And once he has returned from Wisdom and found a positive end state energy, or value, you can associate that feeling into him simply by moving the palm of your hand toward him (don't move it too rapidly, or too close to him; otherwise, you may make him feel threatened!). This movement of your hand, done gently and elegantly, will push the new end state energy inside him, associating him into the emotion.

Let's tie this together with the attention shifting coaching question we built:

"Aside from that anxiety..." [reaching over to the left with your right hand to grasp his old emotion, and moving it over to your right, his left, and his past]...

"...what's everything else you haven't been paying attention to..." [reaching up with your left hand, into the upper right visual field, Wisdom, and showing him the palm of your hand, waiting for him too appear a little confused or to defocus his eyes as he enters Wisdom...]

"...that's truly important to you, now?" [waiting for him to ground into a positive value... as you see him come down into a more positive state...]

"... And where are you feeling that now in your body?" [moving the palm of your left hand gently toward him]

Hopefully this brief summary of John Overdurf's coaching pattern, end state energy, and attention shifting coaching has given you some ideas for how you can coach on your client's right column of his Tree of Life. If you're interested in more details on the coaching pattern, there is a much more detailed explanation in *The Meta Pattern*, by Sarah Carson and Shawn Carson, available at Amazon.com.

For more details on John Overdurf's attention shifting coaching, see John's upcoming book available soon at Amazon.com.

Chapter 11: Coaching the Middle Triad

Coaching the lower triad was all about your client's experience in the moment—tracking what was taking place in the Real World, filtering that information through an appropriate Sensory Model of the World, and using thoughts and emotions proactively to drive behaviors. Coaching in the middle triad is all about making sense of the world—about taking all that sensory information and deciding what you can do with it.

Making sense of the world, and deciding what you want to do with it based upon what's important to you, is determined by your Rules and Energy (values and temperament). In other words, it's all about how your beliefs, your values, your temperament, and so on, consciously, but especially unconsciously, drive your thoughts, emotions, and behaviors.

The middle triad is largely the province of the unconscious mind. Therefore, you can use traditional hypnosis techniques to create change in your client's middle triad. Of course, to do so, you need to have some understanding of how your client's middle triad currently operates and what might serve him or her better. To gain this understanding, you need to teach your client to shine the spotlight of his or her conscious attention on this often completely unconscious area of his or her Tree of Life. Remember that energy generally flows down the Tree of Life from top to bottom. To gain this insight into the client's middle triad, he or she has to reverse the polarity of energy flow by directing attention upward *from* Thought and Emotion *to* Rules and Energy.

Let's take a look at how this works in practice. (For this example, I'll use the pronoun *she* throughout.)

Rules: Identifying Your Client's Rules

The branch of the Tree of Life that contains your client's beliefs is called Rules. As her coach, you are really interested in the beliefs that rule her life. These are the beliefs that show her what her place is in the world, what is possible for her and what is impossible for her, what she has to do and what she shouldn't do.

When you are talking to your client, you can identify these Rules, these beliefs about that place in the world, by listening out for certain words that your client will likely use to label these Rules. These words to listen out for are called "modal operators" and describe possibility, impossibility, and necessity. They include words such as: *can, can't, will, won't, must* (or *have to*), *mustn't, should, shouldn't,* and so on.

A great way to think of modal operators is as a set of walls and magnets within a magnetic maze that defines your client's reality. Picture these words as follows:

Can't: There is a wall or a barrier between your client and what she can't do.

Can: There is no wall or other barrier between your client and what she can do, although there is not necessarily any magnetic force moving her in that direction.

Will: This word implies your client's intention to do the thing she "will do." Of course, this intention may or may not last long enough for her to actually do it!

Won't: This word is similar in some ways to *will*. It implies that your client's intention is to not do something. The big difference is that in expressing her intention to not do something, she is showing you that her *attention* remains on that thing, even though in a negative way.

Must: This word means that there is a totally irresistible magnetic force that would impel your client to do what she must do. It does not, however, mean that she is necessarily within the stream of that magnetic force; it is not unusual to find people who don't do the things they must do!

Mustn't: In contrast to *can't*, *mustn't* doesn't imply that there is any barrier between your client and what she mustn't do. Instead, it more likely implies that certain consequences will take place if she does.

Should: This word implies that there should be a magnetic force moving your client toward the thing she should do. However, it often means that this magnetic force is missing: "I know I should lose weight, but..."

Shouldn't: This one implies that there should be a barrier that prevents your client from doing something. Once again, it often implies that this force or barrier is missing: "I shouldn't eat another doughnut, but..."

Changing Your Client's Rules

Once you've identified your client's rules, you can (together with your client) decide which ones to keep and which ones to change. You can also install new rules. I will give you a few ideas here as to how you might do that.

There are many approaches that you, as the coach, can use to change your client's beliefs about herself and her place in the world (i.e., her rules). I am going to briefly describe one technique from NLP that you can use, which relies on submodalities. If you are familiar with the

NLP practitioner material, you may know this as the "double map across belief change" because it relies on two submodality shifts.

The first step is to identify the limiting belief and ask your client to imagine a specific time when she experienced this. When she has found this event, ask her to describe what she is seeing when she recalls the event, and take note of the submodalities of that internal picture. By this, I mean ask her where the picture is within her visual field, how big the picture is, how far away the picture is, whether she sees herself in the picture or whether she's looking out of her own eyes, whether the picture is framed or unframed, moving or still, and so on.

The next step is to ask her to think of something that used to be true for her but is no longer true. This might be something like an old toy that she used to have as a child that she no longer has. Ask about the qualities of this picture. Because it is no longer true, the picture will ideally have qualities such as being small, far away, dark, and so on. You can then take a picture of the limiting belief and move it into the location, size, and other qualities or submodalities of the thing that used to be true but is no longer true.

The next step is to ask her what she wants to believe instead. Get her to picture this inside her mind.

You can then ask her about something she is certain of. I like to use the statement "The sun will rise in the morning" because it also carries metaphors of a new day and a new start. Ask her about the qualities of this internal picture: size, location, and all the other qualities you have identified as being potentially important.

Finally, you will ask her to move the picture of the new belief into the location, size, and so on of the picture she is certain is true.

You can then test this belief change by reassociating her into the original context and then asking what she believes about herself and her place in the world.

Energy: Identifying Your Client's Values

In this section, I will be talking about values and about other types of personal energy such as chi, or ki. Having said this, bear in mind that a value represents the physical energy in your client's body that comes from thinking about an abstraction. So we are talking about a word that labels an abstraction that is important to your client—something like freedom, love, equality, and so on. Something like freedom is not of value to your client unless the word *freedom* makes her feel a surge of energy within her body.

This is a very important point that is often overlooked in coaching. Clients often tell you what they think their values "should" be, but not what they actually are. So a client might tell you that she values health, and yet many of her behaviors are fundamentally unhealthy, such as not getting enough sleep, taking drugs or excessive alcohol, failing to avoid or address stress, and so on. In this case, although she believes that health should be important to her, it's actually not important to her on an unconscious level. If it were, she would behave differently!

Therefore, in identifying your client's values, you're looking for this positive energy within her body when she talks about values. So if health is truly of value for her, when she talks about health you should see her face light up, her physiology improve, her gestures become more symmetrical, and other markers of a more resourceful state. Incidentally, you should already be able to recognize these markers through the coaching you have done with your client in the lower triad.

You can begin the process of exploring your client's values simply by asking her questions such as, "What's important to you about that? What does that do for you?" Remember, you have to do this in a specific Real World context; in other words, you have to root the Tree of Life within this specific Real World context. Your client's values may be different in the context of work or career than in the context of family or in the context of fun and friendship, and so on. By associating her into a specific context, you will be able to explore her values in that context. You will find values that overlap in several contexts, but you may well find other values that only apply in one context and not in another.

Once you have some responses, some values, you can begin to climb her values chain by asking, "And what's important to you about that? And what does that do for you?" Remember, each value has to be accompanied by a physiological shift that shows you that the word is linked to a feeling in her body.

Now, just because something is important to your client doesn't mean that the value is good for client. For example, if your client values safety, that may sound like a good, healthy value. However, if the value of safety makes your client avoid any risk, including reasonable risks such as the risk of being rejected if she goes on a date, it's likely to be overly restrictive. So once you have discovered your client's values, you may need to "clean them up" to be more useful and supportive.

If you have taken an NLP Master Practitioner course, you're probably familiar with the whole NLP process of values elicitation and values cleanup. A complete discussion of this topic is outside the scope of this book, but I will give you a quick overview again.

Once you have obtained your client's values within a certain context and you have asked what is important about each of these values, to obtain even more values, you can take your client's list of values and ask her to rank them in order.

Once you have an ordered list, you will likely find that some of these values "include" others. So, for example, if your client values health and also values fitness, she may decide that the value of "health" includes fitness for her, meaning that she can't consider herself to be healthy unless she is also fit. This process will allow you to simplify and condense her list of values.

To clean up her list of values, you're essentially looking for three types of values that you might want to help your client change:

Values that are, or may become, contradictory with other values

For example, your client might value "career" and also "adventure." She might be working in a job that offers an attractive career path (satisfying the value of "career") but is also very boring (clashing with the value of "adventure").

One way of dealing with this clash of values is to find a new, higher value that includes both of the clashing values. So you might ask her, "What value includes both "career" and "adventure"?" If she can identify such a value—let's say "self-realization"—the value would include a satisfying career as well as adventuring into new career possibilities, and she can have the best of both worlds.

Values that are "magnetically repulsive" rather than "magnetically attractive"

"Magnetically repulsive" values are values that move people away from something they don't want rather than moving them toward something they do want. Some of these might be fairly obvious; for example, the value of "safety" often implies moving away from "danger" (although it may not). But sometimes these "magnetically repulsive" values are far from obvious; for example, someone may value "love," which sounds positive. But the person may value "love" not because he or she values love in and of itself, but because he or she wishes to move away from loneliness or isolation (dependent personality types, for example).

You'll be able to identify these "magnetically repulsive" values by asking, "What does that do for you?" If you ask this question about a "magnetically repulsive" value, your client may say something like, "Then I won't have to…." It is the negation—"will not"—that gives away the nature of the value. The other way you will be able to tell that you are looking at a "magnetically repulsive" value is that your client is likely to go into a negative state (with the corresponding negative physiology) when he or she talks about the value rather than the positive state you would expect. This may be because the client is unconsciously picturing the thing he or she is magnetically repulsed by.

You have to realize that "magnetically repulsive" values are not necessarily a bad thing. For example, if someone has a healthy fear of heights because he or she values "not falling," this may indeed keep the person safe. On the other hand, someone who has an extreme fear of heights may find him or herself limited in what he or she can do, and where he or she can go, out of proportion to the actual danger. Therefore, you, as the coach, should consider whether or not this "magnetically repulsive" value is serving your client.

There are two main problems that can arise from "magnetically repulsive" values. The first is that moving away from something does not necessarily tell you what to move *toward*. For example, moving away from "being alone" may just result in a series of failed relationships with inappropriate partners. One way of dealing with this sort of "magnetically repulsive" value is to find and install a value around what the client wants instead, and then to find a higher value that includes both this new value and the old "magnetically repulsive" value. For example, if your client has "not being alone" as a value, and if you can find and install a value of "searching for a mutually supportive relationship," you can combine these two into something like "not being alone by searching for a mutually supportive relationship." This will allow your client to join social organizations or otherwise engage in activities that have the potential to allow him or her to meet a good life partner. Since engaging in these activities will mean that your client is not alone, even if he or she has not yet found the ideal partner, your client will satisfy the entirety of the new combined value in a healthier way.

The other problem of "magnetically repulsive" values, of course, is that they may prevent the client from doing things he or she would otherwise wish to do. A value of avoiding the pain of rejection may lead to not socializing at all. In this case you, as the coach, may wish to help your client find a new way of achieving the goal of the value. So, for example, the pain of rejection might be avoided by having a strong self-image.

Values that clients decide they would rather change, or change the relative importance of

This may involve making one value more important than another, or less important. Changes in the ordering of values may have significant consequences for your client, and therefore you should check for ecology before you help your client plan to make such a change.

Values, at least in the way we are describing them here, represent words that are linked to feelings in the body. We can therefore change the relative importance of values by changing the submodalities associated with these feelings. To do this, take your client's list of values, ranked in order of importance, and ask him or her about the quality of the feeling associated with each. So, for example, you can discover:

- The size of the feeling: whether one is larger or smaller than the other
- The location of the feeling: whether one is higher in the body than another
- The temperature of the feeling: whether one is warmer or cooler than the other
- The movement of the feeling: whether one is moving faster or slower than the other
- The weight of the feeling: whether one weighs more or less than the other

What you are ideally looking for is a submodality that changes consistently across the range of values. So, for example, if your client feels the feelings associated with each value in different parts of his or her body, with the most important value felt in the head, the next most important felt in the throat, the third most important in the chest, and the fourth most important felt in the stomach, you should be able to change the relative importance of the values simply by asking your client to move that value up or down within his or her body.

Once again, I want to make the point that ecology is very important. The unconscious mind has a reason for ranking your client's values in the way it does. Just because your client's conscious mind decides that he or she would prefer a different order for the values doesn't mean that the unconscious mind will necessarily agree!

Integration Through the True Unconscious

The True Unconscious is the part of the client's unconscious mind that takes in all the information from the world around him or her and makes sense of that information in light of his or her beliefs and values, i.e., turns it into meaning and then converts that meaning into emotions, thoughts, and most particularly behaviors and actions in the Real World. Thus the True Unconscious is the pivotal central point that turns experience into action, and action into experience.

Once you have "cleaned up" the client's Rules and Energy (values) using the techniques described above, you can integrate these changes into his or her emotions, thoughts, and behaviors using the power of the True Unconscious. The simplest way to do this is using classical hypnosis, if you are hypnosis trained. To do this, you could use the following steps:

1. Induce trance in the client.
2. Remind the client of the new Rules and values.
3. Associate the client back into the context while holding these Rules and values.
4. Ask the client what he or she sees and hears, and what he or she feels, in this context, with these new Rules and values.
5. Ask the client what he or she is paying attention to in the context.
6. Repeat for other similar contexts until the integration generalizes.

Chapter 12: Left Column Coaching

The left column of the Tree of Life represents the cognitive aspects of personality. It's not really correct to say this is "left brain" because, for example, "thoughts" can be words, which are left brain, but can also be pictures and sounds, which are more whole brain. So perhaps it's more accurate to say that the left column is cognitive, and the right column is somatic or bodily feelings.

In this chapter, I will discuss how you can coach your client using aspects of the left pillar, which runs from the Real World through Thought, into Rules (including beliefs), and up through Archetypes.

NLP Coaching as an Example of Left Pillar Coaching

Dr. Richard Bandler, the cofounder of NLP, provides a good example of this sort of coaching in many of his demonstrations. Dr. Bandler will first ask his client about how he or she is thinking, including the submodalities of his or her thoughts, meaning the qualities of the pictures and sounds used to create the thoughts. You might ask questions like:

- Where do you see that picture?
- How close is it?
- How big is it?
- Do you see yourself in the picture, or are you looking at it through your own eyes?

- Is the picture moving or still?

These are all aspects of the visual picture that in NLP are referred to as visual submodalities. To be clear again, submodalities are the qualities of an internal sensory experience, in this case, a picture. Dr. Bandler then might begin to ask the client to change the submodalities, for example, moving a problematic thought-picture farther away while moving a more positive picture closer. This sort of pattern is often called a Swish pattern in NLP.

If the client has difficulty making one of these changes, Dr. Bandler might move up to beliefs (in the branch of Rules). For example, he might do a "map across" pattern to change a client's belief about him- or herself. Or he might move up to the level of reimprinting and make an identity-archetype change in the client.

Using Left Pillar Coaching in a Systematic Way

As always, the first step in the coaching process is to ground the client in his real-world experience. (For this example, I will use the pronoun *he* throughout.) You do this by asking the opening question and the Real World questions:

Opening Question:

- "What do you want to work through?"

Real World Questions:

- "Tell me about the last time and place you experienced this. Where are you? What are you seeing? What are you hearing? What's happening?"

Accessing the Client's Thoughts About the Problem

Assuming you are coaching your client in your office, his experience of the last time and place he had the problem is likely to be a memory (unless he answers the question by saying, "I'm experiencing it right now!"). This means that he will be experiencing the issue by "thinking" about it. He might see a picture of the event in his head, including hearing what was happening at that time, talking to himself about it, and reexperiencing the feelings he felt in his body.

Once you are able to track the nature of your client's thoughts (and feelings), you can change the thoughts by either changing the content of his thoughts or by changing the qualities or submodalities, meaning the way he is thinking these thoughts.

Let's consider a quick example to show you what I mean. Suppose you have a client who has a difficult relationship with somebody, let's say a colleague at work. There's likely to be something this other person does that draws your client's attention—some behavior that your client finds irritating or intrusive in some way. Because of this, it's likely that when you ask your client about his thoughts and his internal picture of that person, you will find:

- He has a picture that is centered on a person, and probably the one aspect of that person, that he finds most annoying.
- The image of the other person is probably big and close to him—much closer than the other objects in the scene. We can say that the other person is the foreground of his experience, and everything else is the background.

To change his experience of that person, we can change the content of the internal picture, the qualities (submodalities) of the internal picture, or both.

Foreground-Background Switch

One good way of changing both content and submodalities at the same time is to do a technique from HNLP called the "foreground-background switch." When a client is fixated on one thing, in this case the other person, it will likely be held in the foreground of his mental pictures, so that if you move it into the background, its power and immediacy are reduced.

In the foreground-background switch, you first find out what the client is focusing on when he is thinking about the problem. Let's call this the foreground. So the foreground might be the face of the person he has a problem with. Everything else in the scene is the background.

You will next ask him to move away whatever is in the foreground so that it becomes the background, and whatever is in the background will move forward and become the foreground. If you think about this in a logical way, it probably doesn't make a lot of sense, but unconsciously it does! What you're really looking for is a widening of the client's attention away from what he is normally focused on.

You'll then ask him to blank the screen and repeat this process—the foreground moving into the background and the background moving into the foreground. Then ask him to blank the screen and repeat, blank the screen and repeat, until he is no longer able to recreate the old, negative feeling.

This technique is often combined with "perceptual position shifts" by inviting the client to see the scene from the other person's position, as a neutral observer or "fly-on-the-wall" position, and from a "whole-system" position, perhaps from outer space. I won't go into these variations here.

Belief Change Using a Submodality "Map Across"

If you find that your client is having difficulty changing how he feels about the situation simply by changing his thoughts about the situation, it may be due to a limiting belief he holds about himself or about the world. For example, suppose you are coaching a client (a woman for this example) who has a fear of speaking in public.

Coach: What do you want to work through?

Client: I'm terrified of speaking in public.

Coach: Tell me about the last time and place you experienced this. Where are you? What are you seeing? What are you hearing? What's happening?

[Notice that the coach shifts into the present progressive tense in order to begin associating the client into the Real World context.]

Client: I'm at work. I'm standing in front of a group of my colleagues, shaking in my boots.

[The client has jumped too far forward in the story. She is already afraid, so the coach needs to back the story up to find the trigger in the Real World context, i.e., the client's Sensory Model of the World.]

Coach: Let's back that up. How do you know it's time for you to feel afraid?

Client: Well, it's my turn to speak, so I stand up and... [The client's head moves back, and a look of terror appears on her face.]

Coach: Wait, hold on—what are you seeing as you stand up?

[The coach has identified the moment when the client sees the Real World trigger but still needs to find out exactly what this is.]

Client: I see everyone's eyes looking at me.

Coach: Let's do an exercise called the foreground-background switch...

[The coach leads the client through the foreground-background switch, but the client reenters the negative state whenever she imagine seeing the eyes of her coworkers.]

Client: … I don't think I can do this…

[The client is telling us that she has a belief about her own ability to "do this." Whether she is talking about speaking in public or making the change is not really important. What is important is that we address this belief. Remember that beliefs lie in the branch of Rules on the Tree of Life because they are governed by "modal operators"—in this case "can't."]

Coach: So you don't believe you can do this. How would you like to change that belief right now, or later?

Client: It would be awesome if I could do that…

Coach: Okay, let's go!

The Belief Change Technique

A belief change using a "map across" of submodalities is a very quick and easy technique to make a change at the level of beliefs (Rules in the Tree of Life). The technique uses "thoughts" and internal pictures to make this change. There are a couple of different versions of this pattern—one involving a simple "map across" and the other involving a double "map across." I will show you the simpler version here.

The first step is to ask the client to make a picture representing the limiting belief. For example, you might ask, "What picture comes to mind when you imagine that you can't do this?"

Once the client has found this picture, you should ask her about the submodalities of the picture. The most important submodality is likely to be the location of the picture, but you should also ask about:

- The size of the picture
- How far away the picture is
- Whether the picture is framed or unframed
- Whether the picture is still or a movie

- Whether the client sees herself in the picture or whether she's looking out of her own eyes
- Whether the picture is bright or dim
- Whether the picture is clear or fuzzy
- Any other submodalities the client particularly notices

Once you have the submodalities of the picture that the client makes when she imagines the negative belief, you can temporarily put that picture on one side.

Now ask her to think about something she is totally confident about or that she totally believes about herself (something positive). Ask about the submodalities of this picture. You'll have to focus on the submodalities that are *different* from those of the limiting belief. Again, the location of the picture may be key.

Now ask her to think about what she will be seeing when she knows for certain that she has been able to make the change and that she is able to do what she wants. Perhaps this is a picture of her colleague smiling and nodding.

Now you are going to ask her to think about the first picture—the one representing the limiting belief. You're going to ask her to send that picture off into the distance so that it becomes small and dark as it moves far away. But the picture is going to be attached to her by a piece of elastic so that after it's moved away, it's going to start to come back again faster and faster.

But—and this is where the change in *content* comes in—when it comes back, it's going to come back as that new picture of her colleague smiling and nodding. And all the submodalities are going to be the same as the confident picture (you, as the coach, will list what these submodalities are).

You, as the coach, will then ask your client to blank the screen and repeat the pattern in order to condition the change.

Sometimes you will have to coach a client who not only has limiting beliefs about herself but also has a negative self-image. A negative self-image is a sort of higher-level belief-thought. So if I have a negative self-image, I don't simply believe, "I'm no good at presenting in front of a group"—I believe something like "I'm just no good," and I see it, or am able to see it, as an "image." So a negative self-image stretches across the branches of Thought (image), Rules (belief), and Archetypes (self).

Now, a person who believes she can't present in front of a group doesn't necessarily believe that she can't change that belief! However, someone who believes that she's no good and she can't do anything may generalize that to a belief that she can't do anything, achieve anything, or change anything, include her own belief!

If your client has this sort of identity-level negative self-image, you should work in the branch of Archetypes. There are several ways of doing this, for example, using Deep Trance Identification (see *Deep Trance Identification*, by Shawn Carson and Jess Marion with John Overdurf, available at Amazon.com) or by using reimprinting.

Working With Archetypes Using Reimprinting

A quick and easy way to work in the branch of Archetypes is to do a reimprinting. An "imprint" is an event, typically from early childhood, in which the child took on an Archetype represented by a parent, older sibling, teacher, or similar role model. Using a reimprinting pattern, you will allow the client to reexperience one or more events from her childhood period. However, the client will reexperience the events from a dissociated perspective, and you, as the coach, will lead the client to add resources to all those present in the situation. These new resources are then incorporated into the memory in a process called "reconsolidation." Reconsolidation means that whenever someone remembers something, the memory is changed based on what is going on as the person remembers it; it's updated to include new information.

Here are the steps of a typical reimprinting (based on the HNLP reimprinting technique developed by John Overdurf):

1. Identify a specific event from early childhood that is relevant to the client's current situation. Sometimes the relevance of the childhood event is not immediately obvious, but what is important is that the client, or the client's unconscious mind, sees the relevance.

2. Keep the client dissociated from the event, as if she were seeing it at a distance. It often helps to make the scene small and far away, as if it were in a miniature theater, on the floor, at the far side of the room.

3. Keeping the client dissociated from the scene, lead her to send additional resources to the younger version of herself in the scene. Do this until the younger version of herself looks resourceful and behaves resourcefully, no matter what the other people in the scene are doing.

4. Lead the client to send additional resources to the other people in the scene. Begin with the least powerful person, until that person is feeling and behaving resourcefully. Work your way up to the most powerful. The reason to do it this way is that this forces each person in the scene to become resourceful in his or her own right. If you began by sending resources to the most powerful person in the scene, so that he or she changed his or her behavior, the other people in the scene might not need to be resourceful.

5. If appropriate, the client can associate into one or more of the characters in the scene. This can be especially important if the client has taken on the feelings or behaviors of that person in the imprint.

6. If you feel it is appropriate, you can then associate the client into her younger self and then grow her up by suggesting that time is passing. This allows her to reexperience each day of her life, from childhood to the present, without that old imprint and with these new resources. This can generalize the change into many different contexts of her life.

Notice that you should be very careful about using this technique if the childhood event is particularly traumatic. It would generally not be appropriate to do this technique, for example, if the events involved some form of abuse, at least until the high-intensity feelings associated with that memory had been cleared using some gentler technique, for example the Tearless Trauma technique from EFT.

Bringing the Change Back into the Real World

If you have made a change in the branch of Archetypes, for example, using reimprinting or Deep Trance Identification techniques, you should bring these changes back into the Real World context by descending back down the Tree of Life.

In practice, you might want to do this using the Lightning Path. But if you simply wanted to stay with the left column, you might say something like:

- Now that you have learned a new way of being, I want you to notice what you're believing about yourself and the world around you [bring the change down into the branch of Rules, including beliefs].
- And when you're believing that [positive belief], what image comes to mind [beginning to bring the change down into Thought]?
- And what are you thinking about [whatever the original presenting issue was], now?
- And as you see [the original trigger], notice how you're feeling now [bringing the change back to the Sensory Model of the World and the Real World context—the faces of the audience. The client's feelings are brought in to check that the changes have been made].

As with any type of coaching, generalization, testing, and future pacing are required in order to cement the change in place.

Chapter 13: Coaching the Upper Triad

The lower triad of the Tree of Life is about your immediate experience in the moment—your experience of the world around you together with your own thoughts and feelings. The middle triad is about the more lasting but also more abstract part of your experience, such as your beliefs and values. So what is the third triad about?

You'll notice, when you look at the Tree of Life, that the lower triad and the middle triad both reach downward, toward the Real World. This is because both the lower triad and middle triad arise from the individual. In contrast, the upper triad points upward, toward heaven or toward God, because it's about the energy that comes from a higher plane—not about the individual.

In this sense, the experiences of the upper triad appear to be outside of our control as individuals. The one resource that is needed more than any other when you and your clients are working in the upper triad is trust. You need to trust that the universe is indeed working out as it should, and that the Source is providing you with opportunities to grow, even when events happen that you weren't expecting and perhaps that you're not enjoying right now.

The Source represents those opportunities and disasters and life-changing events that the universe throws in our direction. The Void represents an opportunity to find a uniquely creative, new way of viewing the universe—a way that is not already contained in our experience. And while we may be familiar with archetypal experiences of those individuals whom we see on television or in the movies, or that we read about in books, there are experiences that are shared with everybody on the planet, not just you as an individual. Nevertheless, if you want to truly control your own life, no matter what happens, you have to be comfortable visiting the upper triad.

There are two ways of navigating the upper triad. You can move from the top down (from Source to Void to Archetypes). Or you can move from the bottom up (from Archetypes to Void to Source). We'll talk about each of these in turn.

Moving Down the Upper Triad from the Source

You will know that your coaching client (a woman, for this example) is moving down the upper triad because she will tell you about some amazing, life-transforming event she has just experienced. This event comes from the Source branch of the Tree of Life. The event may seem, on the face of it, either completely positive or completely negative. So it may be an opportunity for a new career, relationship, or travel, or it may be the loss of a loved one, the breakup of a relationship, the loss of a job or business, or being diagnosed with an illness.

Whatever this event is, it will be something that was totally outside the expectations of your client before she experienced it. Now your client has to decide how to react, but, like Donnie in *The Big Lebowski*, she has "no frame of reference." The first thing you can do as her coach is to allow her to reorient herself to this changed reality. Bear in mind that she may have no frame of reference in which to do this, so that initially any meaning she makes may be inappropriate. You, as the coach, need to hold Wisdom open long enough for her unconscious mind to find an appropriate meaning. To do this, you need to offer your client three things:

- Sufficient uncertainty about her own initial reaction that she doesn't close herself off to other possibilities

- A suggestion that she explore each and every possible meaning that could be made from the situation
- A suggestion that she use her deepest, most profound values to guide her

You may recognize these from Chapter 10, when I talked about using John Overdurf's attention shifting coaching to lead your client up into Wisdom.

Leading your client down from the Source into Wisdom

So you might say something like:

"This is not something that happens every day, and you can't be sure what it means… yet. There's a very good chance that whatever you think it means right now, it will turn out to mean something entirely different. What I suggest you do is to allow your mind to drift over any and all possible meanings, and in particular focus on what's really important to you now… about what happened…"

What you're looking for is for your client to begin to drift in the ocean of possibilities that have been opened up to her by this unexpected event. If she decides too quickly, you might want to encourage her to allow her unconscious mind more time:

"It might be that, but then again it might not. You want to be sure that you… fully and completely consider each and every possibility, that this is anything except what you've already thought of, to the extent that it could reveal what… is really important to you now…"

Leading your client from Wisdom into Archetypes

As your client has spent some time in Wisdom, it may be time for you to lead her into the branch of Archetypes. You might say to her:

"Who would you have to be to deal with this event in the way that will lead you to… what's most important to you now?"

If your client can find the appropriate archetype (it could be her past self, her future self, her ideal self, or somebody else entirely), you can use this archetype to build an entirely new Tree of Life to help your client deal with this new situation. So if your client replies:

"I'd need to be Wonder Woman to deal with this!"

... she has provided you with an archetype that on an unconscious level she believes has the character, the power, the emotional resources, and the intellect to cope or to take advantage of the opportunity. You can therefore begin to explore these conversationally:

"What would be important to Wonder Woman in this situation? What would Wonder Woman be believing about herself in the situation? How would Wonder Woman feel in this situation? What would Wonder Woman be thinking in this situation? What would Wonder Woman be focusing on in the situation?"

Or, if you're familiar with Deep Trance Identification, you could lead your client into trance and work in a trance space.

Moving Up the Triad from Archetypes to Source

The other way of coaching within the upper triad is to move up from Archetypes to Source. This can be an interesting way of coaching if your client wants to "be" somebody other than who she is but does not necessarily have an obvious strategy to achieve that dream. In this case, you can try the following approach.

Associating your client into the branch of Archetypes

You can work in the upper triad by first associating your client into the branch of Archetypes and then using this energy to stimulate the Source to *create* unexpected opportunities.

161

First of all, you can associate your client into who she wants to be—her own ideal future self. As usual, to associate her into this state, you, as the coach, should shift into present-tense language and ask her about her sensory experience:

"I want you to imagine that you have realized your dream… Where are you? What are you seeing? What are you hearing? What are you feeling?"

You want to lead your client into a fully associated sensory experience of her dream. You should also ask her about the timescale. "When is this? How do you know—do you see a calendar?"

Research shows that if somebody associates into his or her dream, he or she is actually less likely to achieve it! Given all the talk about *The Secret*, this may sound counterintuitive, but your unconscious mind can't tell the difference between something that's real and something that's strongly imagined. Therefore, if your unconscious mind believes that you've already achieved your dream because you strongly imagine it, it might not be prepared to take the steps necessary to achieve it in reality.

So, once you've associated your client into her dream, you need to disassociate her from that by telling her to float out of that experience and look at it as if she were seeing herself in a picture or movie. She should then move that picture into her future.

Trigger the dream using the power of Wisdom

Now your client can see her dream—her outcome—waiting for her in the future. If this outcome is something that she can achieve by taking certain specific steps, you can move down the Tree of Life by:

• Making sure that is something she really wants. You can do this by traveling through the branch of Energy and getting in touch with her values.

- Making sure she believes she can achieve it and that she deserves it. You can do this by traveling to the branch of Rules.
- Making sure she has the necessary emotional resources, such as motivation and confidence, to go for it. Do this by traveling to the branch of Emotion.
- Making sure she maintains a picture of herself in the future and that she can also picture herself taking those steps to get to that picture, or at least the smallest next step on that path. To do this, you will lead her to the branch of Thought.
- Making sure she knows how to bring that vision into reality. This knowledge will be of the form, "If I do X, then Y is likely to happen." This is in the branch of her Sensory Model of the World.
- And making sure that she actually takes action (in the Real World).

However, if her dream seems impossible, she will need a little help from God or from the universe, i.e., from the Source (whatever she perceives the Source to be). To activate the Source, you first have to step into Wisdom. To step into Wisdom, you have to make a distinction, and that distinction has to be different from anything that you've done before. What does this mean? How do you do this?

You, as the coach, can do this using the emotional energy your client has generated in the branch of Archetypes. The technique I am about to describe comes from John Overdurf's work on Next Smallest Step coaching. As before, you're going to associate your client into her dream, asking her, "Where are you? What are you seeing? What are you hearing? How are you feeling?" Then you're going to ask your client to float out of that picture and put it in her future. Then you're going to ask her:

"What's the next small step to move you in the direction of that dream?"

In this case, you're not looking for a practical step. For example, if your client wants to be a movie star, the next smallest step is probably not "Find an agent." Instead, like Jim Carrey, it might be something like "Write myself a check for $1 million." Identifying, and then taking, this kind of step activates the power of the Source. The universe will then start to manifest on your client's behalf.

Please bear in mind that your client actually needs to take this step. And then she has to take another step, and then another step.

It's like the story about the man who prays to God to win the lottery. Each week he prays to win, but he never wins. Finally, as an old man, he dies and goes to heaven. Meeting God, he asks, "Why did you never grant my prayer?" To which God replies, "You could've at least bought a lottery ticket." People who don't take action toward their dreams are not going to achieve them. Sometimes people can achieve their dreams by plugging away day after day, doing exactly what is necessary. But sometimes it takes divine genius to help!

Of course, there's no guarantee that appealing to the Source in this way will make your client's dreams come true. But it will almost certainly make her life more interesting!

Chapter 14: Tree of Life Coaching as an Organic Process

Your Tree of Life is not a sculpture that you create, and once created, is frozen in time. Instead, your Tree of Life is a living, breathing, changing, organic life force that surrounds you, guides you, and creates meaning in your life. Each day, your Tree of Life is different from how it was the day before, just as you are different from the "you" of yesterday, and the "you" of tomorrow will be different from the "you" of today.

The true beauty of Tree of Life Coaching is that it embraces the organic nature of human experience. It doesn't turn you into your ideal self—someone you will never be. Instead, it recognizes that there's no such thing as perfection. It allows you to grow, to change, and in doing so to become even more of who you are, and who you can be, without losing sight of your humanity.

Trees that don't allow for the possibility of new growth become rigid and are blown down in the next storm. The trees that are flexible and that adapt to changing conditions are the ones that survive.

What does this mean for Tree of Life Coaching? The good news is that you, as the coach, can use Tree of Life Coaching with your client for as long as he or she remains your client. You become a coaching arborist, tending to your client's Tree of Life. The bad news is that you, and your client, have to be on the lookout for what's not working

165

in his or her life. Sure, you can celebrate success, and you should do so, but you should also be on lookout for exceptions to success—for apparent "failures" that are actually lessons to be learned. And you should lead your client to incorporate these lessons into his or her Tree of Life.

This is not as easy as it sounds, for two reasons. Reason number one is that, as human beings, we tend to notice things that reinforce our current view of reality, and we ignore anything that contradicts this reality. You have probably experienced this with coaching clients who "can't change"; rather than focusing on the change they want, they focus on all the reasons they haven't been able to change in the past and the reasons they won't be able to change in the future.

Reason number two is that it can be emotionally painful to notice and examine things that didn't work out as well as we would have liked. In NLP, we have a phrase: "There's no such thing as failure—there is only feedback." This means that any time you apparently "fail," it is actually an opportunity to learn and grow. A great example of this is Thomas Edison, who was once asked what it felt like to have failed a thousand times to invent the light bulb, to which he replied he had not failed a thousand times, and he is not even failed once; instead, he had discovered a thousand ways not to make a light bulb! It's a great story! But this mindset can be difficult to maintain without specific tools.
One great way of keeping track of how well your Tree of Life is working out for you is embedded in the BEAT System we examined in Chapter 9. Between the "A" and the "T" of the BEAT lies a moment of mindfulness that allows you to use your sensory Awareness to compare the Real World with your expectations (represented by an image or movie that you are holding in your "T" = Thought).

To avoid simply seeing what you want to see, or what you expect to see, you need to open up your senses as much as possible. This is a form of mindfulness. The best way to do this is using the open focus states described in this book. If these two images—what you see in the Real World and what you were expecting or hoping to see in your

166

mind's eye—are the same, your Tree of Life is keeping pace with reality.

It's important to note that it is not always a good thing for your client's Tree of Life to keep pace with reality. For example, you may have a client who believes himself to be a failure and has this expectation confirmed by feedback from the Real World. His Tree of Life is keeping pace with reality, but it's probably not the reality he would like to create for himself!

I will assume, for the purposes of this discussion, that your client is familiar with the BEAT and is making positive and resourceful pictures about the presence of the future using her working memory. So, if your client has a *positive* picture about the future she wants, held in her working memory, and the reality that she sees with her senses matches that picture, her Tree of Life is working out well. If not, it's time for her to update her Tree of Life. To do this, your client has to be aware of what her Tree of Life is at any moment in time:

- What is her Sensory Model of the World? Is she "at cause," meaning is she creating the world around her? Or is she "at effect"?
- What images and meaning is she holding in her working memory?
- Does she have control over her own emotional state? What is she feeling?
- Do her Rules create or restrict possibilities? Is she driven to do those things that are most important to her?
- What is important to her in that moment?
- What memories and other archetypal experiences are shaping her world at this moment?

If that Tree of Life is not working out for her, one of the branches will need to be changed. This may be a slight pruning, or her entire Tree may need to be chopped down and another one grown in its place!

And it all starts with this one simple question: is that what I was hoping for, what I was imagining? If not, what's different? It is the Real World that gives us a "reality check"! And this reality check is the starting point for a whole new Tree of Life.

Chapter 15: Individual Branches and Pathways on the Tree of Life

As you can see from images at the beginning of this book, the Tree of Life consists of ten branches connected by twenty-two pathways.

In the chapters that follow, I will give a brief description of each of the branches. I've included this section at the end of the book, rather than at the beginning, because the power of Tree of Life Coaching lies in the integration of all the branches. If you consider the branches separately, you just have another system with ten "characteristics" for each client rather than one unified Tree of Life. Having said this, it is important that you understand what lies on each of the branches.

In each chapter, I will tell you what that branch is called in Tree of Life Coaching as well as its Hebrew name in Kabbalah and the English translation of the Hebrew name. By the way, there are a number of different spellings of the Hebrew names for the branches, so you may find different spellings if you research the Tree of Life on the Internet or in other books.

I will also tell you what the branch "means" in Tree of Life Coaching and offer you an "Experience" of each branch. I will also give a brief explanation of the meaning of that branch in the Kabbalah to the extent that I feel this is useful. However, this is not intended to be a book about Kabbalah, and in any case, there is no one agreed-upon meaning for each branch. If you want to know more about the Tree of

Life in Kabbalah or in Christian mysticism, there are several great resources online, including, of course, the ubiquitous and omniscient Wikipedia.

I will also explain exactly where the branch lies in the Tree of Life, the pathways that connect it to other branches, and how those pathways can be used to direct energy around the Tree of Life. This is great information because it allows you to change some aspect of your client's experience that lies in one branch of the Tree of Life by making a change in another branch and then directing the energy flow to the first branch. For example, you can change how someone thinks about an issue by changing how he or she feels about the issue and then asking the person what he or she thinks about the new feeling!

As a final point, if you're interested in the Tarot, the branches correspond to the pip cards (with the ace representing the Source, down to the ten representing the Real World), and the twenty-two pathways correspond to the twenty-two cards in the Major Arcana. I won't be discussing this correspondence but would refer interested readers to Isabel Kliegman's book *Tarot and the Tree of Life* from Quest Books.

Chapter 16: The Real World – Malkuth - The Kingdom

The Real World lies at the base of the Tree of Life. It's what you see, and hear, and feel, every moment of every day.

Experience 1

Stamp your foot on the floor. That's the Real World.

Experience 2

Think about some positive emotion you experience in your life—something like confidence or joy or love. Now ground that emotion in your body by beginning to notice when your body feels it—in your heart, or in your chest or your stomach, or perhaps in your hands. Just notice where in your body you feel that emotion.

Now, as you begin to feel that emotion, think back to the last time and place you experienced it. Where are you? See that scene through your own eyes and hear it through your own ears. What is happening around you? What are you doing?

By reexperiencing things in this way, as if you were seeing and hearing them right now, you begin to stimulate the path that lies between emotions and the Real World. Stimulating any pathway like this strengthens it. Like walking a path through a forest, each time you walk the path, it becomes wider and easier to traverse. I will talk more about the pathways leading into and out of each branch at the end of the discussion of that branch.

The Real World You Experience Is Not Real

Of course, the Real World we *experience* is not really "real." There is a Real World out there, but we don't experience the Real World—we experience the world as filtered through our senses. Our senses carry out a number of different processes to make our sensory experience of the world appear smooth and seamless. These processes include:

Deletion

Your senses simply delete from your awareness any information that is not considered to be relevant to your current experience. For example, you may not be aware of the feeling of the clothes you are wearing on your skin, at least until I brought it to your attention, because as soon as you have dressed, the fact that you remain dressed is not relevant. On the other hand, you will automatically become aware if a flying insect lands on your skin because your unconscious is primed to make you aware of something that might bite or sting you, even though the insect weighs a tiny fraction of the weight of your clothing.

Your sensory memory ("episodic memory") works in a similar way. If you consider the last journey you took, whether you walked or drove to the office or took the train, you probably don't remember all the details of that journey. This is especially true if you take the same route on a regular basis because your brain simply deletes any information that is "the same as before." So your memories also delete information.

Distortion

Your brain will also distort your sensory experience of the world so that it "makes sense." An easy way to experience that right now is to tap your fingers on the table in front of you (you can tap your fingers

172

on your knee if there is no table). As you do so, you will feel the tap through your fingertips, hear the sound of the tap with your ears, and see your fingers hitting the table with your eyes. When do all these different events take place? You'll probably experience them all taking place simultaneously—after all, they do. But the actual sensory information is traveling to your brain, and being processed by your brain, at different speeds. The signal from your fingers has to travel from the nerves in your fingertips, up through your hand and into your arm, up your arm and into your spine, and then up your spine and into your brain. In contrast, you see your fingers tapping on the table because the light (traveling at the speed of light) enters your eyes and moves through your optic nerves to your visual cortex, and the sound of the tapping travels at the speed of sound to your ears. If your brain were simply recording these experiences as the signals arrived, you would sense each of these signals at a slightly different time. Instead, your brain slightly distorts time so you sense these things as taking place simultaneously.

Your brain tricks you with all sorts of other distortions as well, most of which are not as obvious as the finger tapping, and you often have no way of checking them. Your brain may make up events that didn't actually take place, for example. As I'm writing this, Brian Williams, the newscaster, has just been put on an extended leave of absence for "making up" stories about his experiences. It is certainly not beyond the realm of possibility that Mr. Williams was actually fooled by his own brain into believing these distortions.

Generalization

Your brain also goes through a process of generalization, filling in the gaps in your actual knowledge.

An easy way to experience this is to extend your arms straight in front of you and bend your wrists up so you're looking at the backs of your hands. Now begin to wriggle your fingers. As you do so, begin to move your hands apart while keeping your eyes straight ahead, and notice that you can still see your fingers moving as you do so. When your arms are fully extended to each side, there will be a point where your hands actually "disappear" and you can no longer see your fingers wriggling. This is because your eyes can only see a little more than 180 degrees from your left side to your right side, if your eyes are pointing straight ahead. Once your hands are outside of this visual field, they can no longer be seen.

After you have tried this exercise, answer the following question: What did your hands disappear into? Did they disappear into blackness? Or did they simply disappear into the "background" of the room? What you'll find is that they disappeared into the background; you do not have a black ring of darkness around your visual field! In fact, your brain makes up a background that is "the same as" the rest of the room around you, and your hands disappear into this made-up background!

Another type of generalization occurs because your brain is continuously trying to make sense of things by experiencing them as "the same as" other things that they are functionally similar to. That's why all toothbrushes look the same, yet your toothbrush looks different from your spouse's toothbrush. All toothbrushes are functionally the same because they all brush teeth. Yet your toothbrush is not the same as your spouse's toothbrush because your toothbrush brushes your teeth, and your spouse's toothbrush does not. You are being fooled by this type of generalization if you ever find yourself saying something like, "All ... are ...." Unfortunately, this kind of generalization can also lead to various types of bigotry.

Meaning in Kabbalah

In the Kabbalistic Tree of Life, this point is called Malkuth, meaning the Kingdom. It represents the real physical world—a world full of the mystery and magic of God's creation.

Meaning in Tree of Life Coaching

174

In Tree of Life Coaching, the Real World represents the context in which the client experiences a problem or wants to create a change. It represents the "where and when" of the problem.

It is not as simple as you might think to identify the client's "context" for a change he or she wants in his or her life. This is because of the mental processes discussed above: deletion, distortion, and generalization. For example, if a male client comes in with a problem—"I am depressed"—and you ask him where and when the problem takes place, he might well say, "It happens all the time—I always feel depressed." What he is doing is deleting any times and places when he felt anything but "depressed," and generalizing his experience out to be "depressed at all times and in all places."

In order to fully utilize Tree of Life Coaching, you, as the coach, have to ground the client's experience into the Real World before you move farther up the tree. Without this grounding there will be no roots, and without roots you will not be able to grow and nurture a new Tree of Life for him.

In order to ground his Tree of Life, you have to ask him to describe a specific time and place where he experiences the problem and where he wants to change. To do this, you ask questions such as:

"If it happens all the time, it should be easy to choose one time and place. Tell me about that…"

Pathways

The Real World is connected upward to the branches of the Sensory Model of the World, Thoughts, and Emotions.

This means that the Sensory Model of the World we hold to be true directly impacts our thoughts and emotions as well as our behavior in the Real World. We represent this cause-and-effect by imagining the flow of energy moving down these pathways.

At the same time, the energy flows both ways in any pathway in the Tree of Life. This means that what happens in the Real World directly impacts what we are thinking about and how we are feeling (our emotions); you'll notice this the next time you stub your toe! Real World experiences also hopefully impact our Sensory Model of the World—this is called learning!

Chapter 17: Sensory Model of the World – Yesod - The Foundation

Having left the Real World, we now move straight up to the next branch of the Tree of Life—the Sensory Model of the World. The Sensory Model of the World is the world we actually experience on a day-to-day basis. We often mistake it for the Real World, but in fact it differs, sometimes significantly, from the Real World. Sometimes these differences are minor and sometimes they're huge, depending upon how rigidly we have set our "filters." I'll talk about filters a little later in this section.

The branch of the Tree of Life representing your Sensory Model of the World lies directly above the Real World and is closely related to the Real World. It represents the images, sounds, and feelings we experience when we turn our attention outward.

However, we don't see everything that takes place around us, we don't hear everything that takes place around us, and we don't feel everything that takes place around us, at least on a conscious level. Our conscious mind picks and chooses what we will actually experience on a sensory level.

Also, much of what we believe we see, hear, and feel does not actually originate in the Real World; rather, it originates in our Sensory Model of the World. There is a lot of research and evidence about this, particularly in the context of eyewitnesses to crimes and traffic accidents. For example, eyewitnesses to a traffic accident will estimate speed as being higher if they are asked questions such as "How fast was the first car going when it smashed into the second car?" versus "How fast was the first car going when it bumped into the second car?" Changing one word of the question will change the experience. This is called expectation bias in psychology, meaning we see, hear, and feel what we expect to see, hear, and feel.

Experience

Let's consider a quick Real World example.

Take a look around you and think *vertical*—everything represented by a straight line pointing upward. This may be the leg of a chair or table, the side of a window, a lamppost or street sign, even a person who is standing up. Just look around you as you filter for everything that is vertical.

Now switch your attention to everything that's *horizontal*. This may be the surface of a table or the seat of a chair, a windowsill or a curtain rod, the top of a door, or the edge of a shelf. Simply filter for everything that's horizontal.

What you may have experienced in this exercise is that your sensory experience of the world depends upon the filters you choose to put upon it. When you filter using the word *vertical*, you will tend to see things that are vertical, and when you filter using the word *horizontal*, you will tend to see things that are horizontal. You can experience other versions of this exercise by thinking *blue*, thereby "asking" your eyes to look for things that are blue, and then thinking *red*, "asking" your eyes to look for things that are red. You'll see that your senses are seeking out those experiences you ask them to seek out.

Why Lucky People Are Lucky

There is a fascinating piece of research in which people are asked to find certain words in a newspaper. If they're able to find those words, they are paid a small amount of money. Inside the newspaper is a full-page advertisement that says if they take the advertisement to the researcher who is sitting at the front of the room, he will give them $100.

Before they start the task, they are also asked whether or not they consider themselves to be "lucky."

When researchers carry out this experiment, they find that some people see the advertisement and claim the $100, while other people are so focused on looking for the individual words they have been told to find that they totally miss the "big picture" possibility.

The interesting thing about the experiment is that the people who find the advertisement and claim the $100 reward are the same people who regard themselves as being "lucky." The people who are fixated on finding individual words and who miss the big picture are the people who regard themselves as being "unlucky." The lesson to be drawn from this experiment is that lucky people have set their internal filters wide and hence see the opportunities that exist around them. Unlucky people have set their filters in a different way—more narrowly—and fail to see opportunity when it arises.

Meaning in Kabbalah

In the Kabbalah, this point is called Yesod, meaning the Foundation. Yesod is often taken as meaning imagination or intuition. It's how we relate to the world around us by "imagining" what it's like rather than by observing what it's really like.

Meaning in Tree of Life Coaching

In Tree of Life Coaching, we take this branch of the Tree of Life—this Sensory Model of the World—as representing how your clients perceives the world is working. If you're familiar with NLP, you can think of this branch, for you, as representing:

- Any "cause-and-effect" relationship in which you are either "at cause" or "at effect"
- Any "complex equivalence," especially to the extent that there is an implied cause-and-effect embedded with it
- Your sensory experience that arises from the filters you place on your senses, including, in particular, filters arising from the above cause-and-effect relationships

Let's examine each of these in turn, starting with cause-and-effect.

Cause-and-Effect

Cause-and-effect relates to how one event causes another event to happen. I turn on the switch, and my action *causes* the light to come on. Getting a pay raise *causes* me to be happy. Being in front of an audience *causes* me to be afraid.

For each of these, there is a cause and an effect. When I turn on the light, I am the cause (we often say "at cause"), and the light is the effect ("at effect"). The pay raise is "at cause" and my state (in this case, happiness) is "at effect." The audience is "at cause" and my state (in this case, fear) is "at effect." As a tip, it's generally better to be at cause than at effect, unless everything causes you to be happy!

Cause-and-effects in my Sensory Model of the World are not only created by reality—they also create reality. Remember, energy flows both down and up the pathways in the Tree of Life.

So for example, my Sensory Model of the World might include one of the following:

- If I work hard, I'll get ahead (working hard *causes* me to succeed).
- Hard work is its own reward (working hard *causes* me to be happy).
- It doesn't matter how hard you work—the game is rigged and you can't get ahead (hard work does *not* cause me to succeed).

180

In the first two statements, my state of success (in the case of the first statement) or my happiness (in the case of the second statement) is caused by my work. In the third statement, my lack of success is caused by the system.

None of these statements are true by themselves, and none of these statements are false by themselves. Each statement is true or false depending on the context, i.e., depending upon what actually happens in the Real World. One person may work hard and become wildly successful, a second person might work hard at something he or she loves that carries little financial reward, and a third person might work hard and remain stuck in a dead-end job. It just depends. So they're not statements about the Real World as such—they're simply alternative models of the world.

And it's just as accurate to say that these types of statements can *create* the Real World for your coaching client, at least to the extent that your client actually believes them. Somebody who believes that if they work hard they'll get ahead is very likely to actually work hard and therefore is *more likely* to get ahead. Somebody who believes that hard work is its own reward will also work hard, but perhaps they will focus on something they love rather than something that is financially rewarding. Finally, the cynic who believes that the game is rigged is unlikely to bother working hard at all and will be rewarded accordingly (whether or not the game is rigged!).

When you are coaching clients, you'll find that their lives and their beliefs are full of these models of reality, these models of the world. Your client might say something like, "My boss intimidates me," meaning that his or her boss makes your client feel intimidated.

In coaching, you should always seek to put your client "at cause." It is not that his or her boss makes your client feel intimidated—your client makes him- or herself feel intimidated in the presence of the boss. This puts the control of your client's state and emotions in his or her own hands.

Experience

Complete the following sentences:

- X makes me feel Y.
- X makes me do Y.

When you have a couple of these sorts of sentences, ask yourself what would happen if X happened but you actually didn't feel Y, or actually didn't do Y?

Try these:

- X stops me from feeling Y.
- X stops me from doing Y.

When you have a couple of these sentences, ask yourself what would happen if X existed, but nevertheless you did feel Y, or did do Y?

What you'll find is that while there may be consequences of your actions or feelings, nobody is actually *making* you do or feel anything or stopping you from doing or feeling anything other than you, yourself. (Of course, there are exceptions to this in the natural world, such as "Gravity makes me return to Earth"!)

Complex Equivalence

A variation of cause-and-effect, and one that can be even more powerful, is something called "complex equivalence" in NLP. A complex equivalence occurs when I say one thing is "the same as" or identical to another thing. In the coaching context, you might hear your client say, "I have to go to a networking event that's a waste of time" (the event is identical to a waste of time). These types of thoughts or statements can limit your client by closing down possibilities. If the networking event really is identical to a waste of

182

time, it will be impossible for your client to get any benefit from it. After all, if he or she did get even a slight benefit, the activity would not be *identical* to a waste of time. Better to say, "…might be a waste of time" because this at least leaves open the possibility of a benefit.

A complex equivalence is more powerful than a cause-and-effect because there are often cause-and-effects embedded within the complex equivalence, but they exist at an unconscious level. They are therefore more difficult to challenge. For example, if your client tells you that he or she has come to see you because his or her boss is impossible (complex equivalence meaning that the boss is identical to impossibility!), there is probably also an embedded cause-and-effect, perhaps, "My boss is impossible… and that causes me to feel stressed."

Sensory Experience and Sensory Model of the World

Our sensory experience is very closely linked to our Sensory Model of the World. For example, suppose I believe someone *is* angry with me (note that this is a complex equivalence) and people who are angry with me *cause* me to feel intimidated (a cause-and-effect in which their anger is at cause and I am at effect). When that person enters the room, I'm likely to either pay special attention to him or her, looking at the person in case he or she is about to attack me, perhaps, or pretend to ignore the person by looking anywhere but in his or her direction.

Pathways

As I explained in the previous section, the branch representing the Sensory Model of the World is directly connected to the Real World. In fact, the two are so intimately linked that we often mistake one for the other. Our Sensory Model of the World is created by our Real World experiences as energy flows up this pathway, but our Sensory Model of the World also creates much of our reality as energy flows down this pathway.

Moving up the Tree of Life, the Sensory Model of the World is also connected to Thought and Emotion. This means that we make decisions about the world we inhabit (our Sensory Model of the World) based on our thoughts and also based on our emotions. Energy is flowing down these pathways, from Thought and Emotion to the Sensory Model of the World.

At the same time, our Sensory Model of the World causes us to think a certain way and also makes us feel certain emotions. These thoughts and emotions tend to be self-fulfilling in the sense that they create our experience to fit our model of the world. For example, if you have a client with a Sensory Model of the World that includes a cause-and-effect that flying causes him or her to be afraid, your client is likely to "think" of pictures inside his or her mind of turbulence or plane crashes and to feel negative emotions as a result. The client will then find that his or her Sensory Model of the World is indeed "true," as the client does become afraid whenever he or she gets on an airplane.

The Sensory Model of the World branch is also connected to the True Unconscious. Your True Unconscious is perfectly aware of your Sensory Model of the World and uses it to control the rest of your Tree of Life.

There is an old Sufi story about a man who is walking toward a city when he meets the wise man Nasrudin by the side of the road. He stops and asks Nasrudin, "Tell me sir, what type of people lived in the city?" Nasrudin thinks for a moment and responds, "First tell me what type of people live in the city you come from." The traveler replies, "They are all rogues and scoundrels—that's why I left!" Nasrudin tells him, "I am afraid you will find the people in that city the same way." The traveler shakes his head sadly and goes on his way. Shortly afterward, a second traveler walks down the road and he, too, asks Nasrudin, "Tell me, sir, what type of people lived in the city?" Nasrudin thinks for a moment and responds, "First tell me what type of people live in the city you come from." The traveler replies, "Ah, sir, the people from my city are wonderful—they're the kindest, most generous people on the face of the earth!" Nasrudin tells him, "I'm glad to tell you that you will find the people in that city the same way."

Energy flows up from your Sensory Model of the World to your True Unconscious, and you process your experience based upon this. Of course, energy also flows down from your True Unconscious to your Sensory Model of the World, allowing your Sensory Model of the World to be modified by higher branches on your Tree of Life.

Chapter 18: Thought – Hod - Glory

On your Tree of Life, the branch of Thought lies at the bottom of the left-hand column (i.e., for your Tree of Life it lies on your left, but for your client's Tree of Life it lies on his or her left, therefore on your right). It comprises part of the lower triad, which is comprised of the branches of Thought, Emotion, and the Sensory Model of the World.

As such, the branch of Thought lies below the branch of Rules. Remember that energy tends to flow down the Tree of Life (although it can also flow upward). Therefore, we tend to think according to the rules (beliefs) that we hold, even if we are not consciously aware of, i.e., thinking about, those rules and beliefs.

The branch of Thought lies across from the branch of Emotion, which occupies an equivalent place on the right-hand column. This is because the thinking mind and the emotional body are equal parts of one mind-body system. Indeed, individuals who have a certain type of brain trauma that impacts their ability to generate emotions are not able to effectively function in the world.

Experience

Take a moment to notice the thoughts that are passing through your mind...

This is probably quite easy if those thoughts are expressed as words, as self-talk. You may or may not be used to tracking thoughts that arise as pictures, sounds, or other sensory experiences.

Notice any thoughts that arise as something other than a sensory experience... Did you notice any? What were they?

Close your eyes and think about a dog. You may have made a movie or picture of the dog, perhaps the dog you have, or a dog you had as a child, or perhaps a more abstract dog such as Lassie.

Now close your eyes and think about the dog without making a picture or movie. Perhaps you heard the sound of a dog barking.

In any case, now think of a dog without seeing a picture or movie of the dog or hearing any sound that a dog might make. Perhaps you imagined the feeling of petting a dog.

In any case, now think of the dog without seeing a picture or movie, hearing a sound, or getting any sense of touching the dog. Perhaps you imagined the smell of a dog.

Now think about a dog without seeing a picture or a movie, hearing the sound, touching or otherwise feeling the dog, smelling the dog, or tasting the dog (ugh). As you do this, you begin to realize that when we think, we think using our senses.

As human beings, we find it virtually impossible to think other than by using our senses. Even intuition will arise as a "feeling," or a "flash of insight" (visual impression), or as some other sense.

Meaning in Kabbalah

In the Tree of Life of the Kabbalah, this branch of the Tree of Life is called Hod, meaning Glory. Hod is generally taken to represent thoughts in the Kabbalah, exactly the same as in the coaching Tree of Life.

Meaning in Tree of Life Coaching

In the coaching Tree of Life, the branch of Thought represents the various ways we can represent our experience of the world. When we think, we have to think in a sensory way, meaning we have to say something inside our head, or make a picture, or hear a sound. Less commonly, some people "think" by experiencing a smell or taste inside their mind, but we will focus here on visual, auditory (sound), and self-talk "thoughts."

You "think" in this way using a part of your brain called working memory. Working memory is comprised of three parts: a visual part called the "'visuospatial sketchpad" (often a short movie clip, although it could instead be a more abstract picture), an auditory sound loop that goes along with the movie, and the "'title" of the movie. In many ways, the title of the movie is the most important because it gives meaning to the movie.

Of course, we can also think about your sense of touch, or balance, or you might think about a smell or taste. We can also "think" about emotions; I can think that love is a good thing and hate is a bad thing. However, to do so, I have to think in words—"Love is a good thing"—or I have to make some kind of internal picture or movie that demonstrates that love is a good thing. I can also feel the emotion without thinking about it. I can feel love, for example, but for the purposes of the Tree of Life, the feeling of love lies in the branch of Emotion, not in the branch of Thought.

If you have a coaching client who has a recurring problem, there is a good chance that he or she is thinking about things in the wrong way. And the client will be using his or her working memory to do so.

For example, I see a number of clients to have a fear of flying. They come and see me and tell me they have a fear of flying, but for many of them they actually have a fear of crashing. When they get on an airplane, they begin to make movies of the plane crashing. Indeed,

188

some of them begin to make movies of the plane crashing when they buy their plane ticket and sometimes even before that. This is a great way to become afraid of getting on an airplane!

These clients may not actually be aware that they are making these movies until I ask them what they see when they close their eyes. Once they realize that they are making these sorts of movies, they may still be afraid, but at least they understand why they're afraid. Then all they have to do to change their response is to change the sorts of movies they are playing in their working memory.

Fortunately, once you understand that your thoughts are comprised of a short movie with a soundtrack and a movie title, with a little practice your thoughts become very easy to control. You can simply choose what movies you want to play inside your mind, with the soundtrack and title that you choose.

There are a number of subtleties in doing this in an effective way. One of these key points involves the title of the movie. For example, I have a client who played amazing movies inside his head of all the things he wanted to have in his future—the ideal home by the sea with the expensive motorcar and the wonderful family. At the same time, his life was not moving in the direction he wanted. When I asked him what the title of his movie was, he told me, "All the things I will never have." It's no wonder his wonderful movies were not translating into wonderful things in his life!

It's also important not to simply play wonderful Pollyanna movies in your mind of the great things you will have after you have succeeded in reaching your goals. These will not prepare you for the challenges you will face. Therefore, it's also important for you to play movies in which you confront and overcome these challenges so that when you actually face them in real life, you will be prepared.

Pathways

The branch of Thought is linked to both the Sensory Model of the World and the Real World, both of which lie below it. This 'double' linking reflects our tendency as human beings to think about what is going on in the world around us and how that reflects on the workings of the world. For example, you might hear about somebody at work losing his or her job. You might consider about what you heard and then think, "That's not fair." You would be thinking about the Real World conversation you had as well as the fact that in your Sensory Model of the World, what happened was "not fair."

If you want to change your thoughts, you can change the people and things you surround yourself with in the Real World. You can change the places where you spend your time, and you can change the things that you do. Over time, this will change your thoughts. After all, if you hang out in wonderful places, with wonderful people, doing wonderful things, you will tend to have wonderful thoughts.

We all carry around in our heads a Sensory Model of the World. This model tells you how the world works; these rules apply to the world in general, not just your place within the world. When you think thoughts about the world around you, you're probably thinking about your Sensory Model of the World more than the Real World. This is energy flowing from your Sensory Model of the World to Thought. As always, energy can also flow the other way, down from Thought to your Sensory Model of the World. For example, by reading books on philosophy or ethics, you may begin to broaden your Sensory Model of the World.

The branch of Thought in the Tree of Life is connected laterally to the branch of Emotion. Remember that mind and body form one system. What you think impacts how you feel, and your feelings in the moment are reflected in your thoughts.

In HNLP, we say that everything is dependent upon state. The state you are in (in particular, the emotional state) will influence your thoughts, your beliefs, your values, and your very identity. If someone is feeling miserable, he or she is likely to have miserable thoughts, and

190

if the person is feeling anxious, he or she is likely to have anxious thoughts. But when you are feeling happy, you are likely to have happy thoughts. And when you're feeling confident, you are likely to have confident thoughts.

The branch of Thought is also connected to the branch of the True Unconscious. As usual, the True Unconscious is one of the most powerful branches in the Tree of Life because it is directly connected to every other branch (other than the Real World). Working within the True Unconscious using trance work, self-hypnosis, or meditation can strengthen the branch of Thought. This is particularly true when the meditation involves some kind of visualization utilizing working memory (with visual and auditory components and a positive and empowering title), such as compassion meditation.

The branch of Thought is connected directly upward to the branch of Rules. One of the easiest and most powerful ways to adjust the way you think is to adopt a set of positive principles. Many people have principles they learned from their family, their religion, or other early influences. These principles become embedded in the branch of Rules, and the energy flows down from Rules to Thought. If you have thoughts that lie outside of the principles in the branch of Rules in your Tree of Life, you will immediately feel uncomfortable and banish the thoughts from your mind. For example, if you were taught not to steal by your parents, if the thought of stealing ever entered your mind, you would immediately reject it.

Alternatively, if you want to strengthen the rules by which you live, you could do worse than to read an autobiography of someone you admire greatly. These often contain statements of the principles by which the people lived their lives, principles that you too may be able to adopt. Reading such an autobiography can cause energy to flow from the branch of Thought (as you read) to the branch of Rules. And once you have strong guiding rules and principles in your life, these act as the framework within which your thoughts will lie as the energy flows back down to Thought.

191

Chapter 19: Emotion – Netzach – Eternity

We now come to the branch of the Tree of Life representing emotions.

This branch lies at the base of the right-hand column, meaning on your right-hand side for your Tree of Life (your left-hand side if you are the coach facing your client).

Experience

Go inside and notice how you're feeling emotionally. Are you happy? Are you sad? Are you curious? Are you feeling neutral? Notice where in your body you are feeling that emotion. Is it in your chest, in your heart, in your stomach, or in your hands or your feet?

Think of a time when you felt really happy. Perhaps you were with a group of people you care about and who care about you. Were you eating, drinking, laughing, dancing? Step into that experience so you are seeing out of your own eyes, and hearing with your own ears, and feeling with your own skin and your own body. Make the pictures brighter and the sound clearer. Check it and notice how you're feeling now.

Our emotional body is not simply designed to respond to the Real World, but also to respond directly to our thoughts. If we remember a time when we felt great and we really step into that experience, our body will recreate the emotion we felt at that time. You can feel good whenever you want. And once you understand this principle, as a coach you can make your clients feel good as well.

Emotion in the Tree of Life

If you see a tiger in the forest, your brain and body release a cocktail of neurochemicals and physical chemicals such as adrenaline. These chemicals set your brain and body in the optimal "fight or flight" state so that you can best survive the encounter with the tiger. Your heart speeds up, your lungs begin taking in more oxygen, your digestion closes down, and the blood is instead pumped to your arms and legs as well as to your brain to keep you alert. As your body reacts in this way, it sends signals back to your brain telling you that you're ready for fight or flight. You will feel your heart rate increase, you may get butterflies in your stomach if your digestion closes down, and you may feel your arms and legs begin to shake due to the increased blood flow. Your brain places a label on the emotion, perhaps "fear." But the emotion itself (the feeling inside your body) is caused by the flow of chemical and electrical energy through your body.

You feel the emotions in the now. The branch of Emotion is part of the lower triad of the Tree of Life, meaning it is part of our moment-by-moment experience. After all, we can only feel emotions in the moment. (This is in contrast to the branch of Energy, which can have a more long-term effect on your life, for example, through your values.)

The branch of Emotion is directly linked to both the Real World branch and the branch representing your Sensory Model of the World. What this means is that you can be emotionally impacted by something in the Real World or by something in your Sensory Model of the World. As an example, you may have seen a YouTube video that circulated, showing quadruplets babies laughing. No one had to explain to you what this video meant—you simply found yourself laughing along, and your emotions were directly created by what you saw. Contrast that with someone telling you, "I won't be able to see you today, let's reschedule for next week." The emotional meaning of this will very much depend upon your relationship to that person. For example, is the person your lover or your dentist? You will have to consult your Sensory Model of the World branch to determine how you should feel about this!

The branch of Thought balances the branch of Emotion on the other side of the Tree of Life. Our thoughts and emotions act in a feedback loop; if we begin to think negative thoughts, we will begin to feel negative emotions. And if we begin to feel negative emotions, we will begin to think negative thoughts. On the other hand, when we feel good we tend to think positive thoughts, and when we think positive thoughts we tend to feel good. This is called looking at life through rose-colored glasses!

Directly above Emotion lies the branch of Energy. In fact, your emotions are simply labels that your brain gives to the feeling of energy that flows within your body at any moment in time.

And, of course, the branch of Emotion is connected to the branch of the True Unconscious. Your unconscious mind is tracking your emotional state in each moment.

Meaning in Kabbalah

In the Kabbalah, this branch is called Netzach, meaning Eternity. It is often interpreted in the Kabbalah as representing emotions, the same meaning as in Tree of Life Coaching.

Meaning in Tree of Life Coaching

In NLP, and more particularly in HNLP, coaching revolves around teaching clients how to change and control their state. When we say "state," we mean the totality of their experience in any moment in time, but we are primarily concerned with their emotional state. This is so much so that in HNLP we refer to "sorting by state," meaning that, as coaches, we should always be aware of our clients' emotional state. If we are ever unsure what their emotional state is, we will ask them, "What's happening now?"

Being able to track and control the states of the people you interact with is one of the most important skills you can have in life, whether you are a coach, a salesperson, a manager, a teacher, a parent, or just a human being. When you have mastered this skill, you can make people feel good about themselves, at least as long as they are with you. Remember, we are talking about someone's emotional state in the moment, not about whether they are a "happy person" or a "sad person"; these longer-term states (called end states in HNLP) are kept in the branch of Energy.

As a coach, you need to refine the skill of tracking and transforming your client's emotional state in the moment even further, by being able to control the flow of energy that comes from the Real World, and from your client's Sensory Model of the World, into the branch of Emotion.

One way to control the emotional state of your client (a woman, for this example) in your office is to remind her of a time in the past when she felt that emotion and inviting her to step back into that experience. However, this only gets you to the place where you can control your client's emotional state *in your office*. To really help her in the Real World, you need to be able to install a trigger or anchor that will take her back into that positive state at the very moment she needs it. For example, if your client comes to you with a fear of public speaking, it's not enough to lead her into a state of confidence in your office—you have to make sure that state of confidence is available the next time she steps in front of an audience. I will show you how to do this below when I talk about anchoring.

Pathways

The branch of Emotion is joined to the rest of the Tree of Life through five pathways that lead to the branches of Energy, the True

195

Unconscious, Thought, the Sensory Model of the World, and the Real World. If you have a client who suffers from negative emotions, these may be caused by a flow of energy through any one or more of these five pathways. If you, as the coach, want to get your client to transform that negative emotion into a positive emotion, you can use the same pathway (leading to Emotion) or one of the other five pathways.

The easiest way to ensure your client has the emotion she needs at the exact time she needs it—for example, confidence—is to "anchor" the state of confidence on to something that she will see or hear in the Real World context in which she will need the state of confidence. In the example of a client who has a fear of public speaking, you could anchor the state onto the faces of the audience. Through anchoring, you are causing energy to flow from the branch of the Real World to the branch of Emotion.

You can also anchor an emotional state by flowing energy from the branch of Thought *representing* the Real World—meaning imagination—to the branch of Emotion and vice versa. Remember, the unconscious mind is unable to tell the difference between reality and something that is strongly imagined. The first step is to lead your client into a state of confidence and then invite her to *imagine* seeing the faces of her audience. This sends a burst of energy down the pathway from the branch of Emotion to the branch of Thought (as she makes an internal picture of the Real World). You then invite her to blank her internal screen, restimulate that sense of confidence, and invite her to imagine seeing the faces of the audience.

The more you repeat the steps, the stronger that pathway becomes between Emotion-of-confidence and Real-World-of-audience. At some point, this pathway will become so strong that energy will flow easily in the opposite direction, so that simply inviting her to imagine seeing the faces of her audience will *cause* her to feel confident.

One of the principal causes of unhappiness in the world is the difference between expectation and reality. For example, perhaps a male client imagines himself to be rich and famous, and finds himself middle class and unknown outside of his immediate circle of family and friends. Another cause of unhappiness is the meaning we attach to certain events. For example, perhaps your client receives negative feedback at work and takes that to *mean* that he is a failure or that he has no future with the company. Both of these types of issues arise from the client's Sensory Model of the World branch. He imagines that the world should be a certain way and is not, and based on this *meaning* of events (complex equivalence), he creates a map of the world that makes him (cause-and-effect) feel bad.

The key to changing this type of issue is through "reframing." Reframing simply refers to changing the meaning of some event. The simplest way to do this is by saying to your client, "That event doesn't mean X—it actually means Y" and then explaining why this is so.

A great example of reframing comes from a client session that was done by Leslie Cameron Bandler with a client who was married with children and was upset by the fact that her kids and husband left marks on her nice white carpet. She took this as *meaning* that they didn't really care about her; after all, they knew how much she wanted to keep her carpet cleaning (complex equivalence). This meaning cause her (cause-and-effect) to feel unloved. Bandler asked the woman to imagine she was in the house and her carpet was absolutely spotlessly clean, and then pointed out to her that this *meant* that her husband and children were not there and she was therefore alone. This "reframed" the marks on the carpet as *meaning* the woman had her family around her, which *caused* her to feel happy. The marks on the carpet were the same, but her emotional response to them was different because the meaning had changed—her Sensory Model of the World had changed.

The branch of Emotion is linked to the branch of Thought. You may have a client who constantly thinks about (for example, makes pictures of) things that could go wrong in his life. There's a TV ad for DirecTV with a voiceover that says, "When you have cable and can't find something good to watch, you get depressed. When you get depressed, you attend seminars. When you attend seminars, you feel like a

197

winner. When you feel like a winner, you go to Vegas. When you go to Vegas, you lose everything. And when you lose everything, you sell your hair to a wig shop. Don't sell your hair to a wig shop. Get rid of cable and upgrade to DirecTV." When people run these types of thought loops through their heads, not only do they end up selling their hair to a wig shop, but they also feel negative emotions, so that energy is flowing from the branch of Thoughts to the branch of Emotion. The energy also flows in the opposite direction; when you are feeling happy, you tend to think happy thoughts.

The branch of Emotion is linked to the branch of the True Unconscious. The unconscious mind uses emotions to set your mind-body in what your unconscious believes is the optimal state for survival. Unfortunately, our survival over millions of years has depended upon our ability to deal with hungry tigers and other existential threats. For the most part, we no longer face these kinds of threats on a day-to-day basis, but our neurology is still primarily wired to deal with these types of threats. That's why fear and anxiety can still be problems, even though the only thing many of us have to fear is the risk of giving a bad presentation or being turned down for a date. In neuroscience, this leads to a human trait called "negativity bias," meaning we focus more on the negative than the positive as a general rule.

As usual, energy tends to flow down the Tree of Life, for example, down from the branch of Energy into the branch of Emotion. In Buddhism, the energy in your Energy branch is one aspect of your "Buddha nature," meaning how you are as a person. There are many different types of Buddhas—laughing Buddha, sleeping Buddha, teaching Buddha, and so on—and you *tend* to experience emotions that are aligned with your Buddha nature as energy flows down from the branch of Energy to the branch of Emotion.

You can also reverse the direction of this flow. If you spend a lot of time in a particular emotional state, it becomes more firmly wired into your neurology and therefore easier for you to access. A great example of this is Norman Cousins, who claimed that he cured himself of

198

cancer by watching comedy films. By laughing on a daily basis, he made laughter part of his energetic being.

Chapter 20: The True Unconscious — Tiferet — Beauty

We have now reached one of the most important points in the Tree of Life. In fact, this point is so important in the Christian Kabbalah that it is often referred to as the "Jesus Point."

In the coaching Tree of Life, we refer to it as the True Unconscious. It lies in the very center of the Tree of Life, directly above the Sensory Model of the World.

Meaning in Kabbalah

In the Christian Kabbalah, this point in the Tree of Life, referred to as Tiferet, represents Jesus, the Messiah. Tiferet lies at the center of the Tree of Life, a sort of crossroads where all the energy of the Real World, including our thoughts and emotions, meet the more abstract energy of the points above.

Tiferet can also be thought of as the point of balance, lying as it does in the center of the Tree of Life. It balances the emotions and energies of the right column with the thoughts and concepts on the left column. It balances the physical nature of humans—meaning the Sensory Model of the World and the Real World that lies below—with our spiritual nature, which is represented by the Source that lies above.

Meaning in Tree of Life Coaching

As a coach, it helps to be a good hypnotist. And in order to apply Tree of Life Coaching, it is necessary that you understand hypnosis and the unconscious mind. Of course, the unconscious mind is a myth—a metaphor for how the mind actually works, but it is a very useful myth!

Most of what your brain does is outside of your immediate awareness. In fact, it's impossible for you to be aware of most of the things that your brain actually does. For example, if you look at the world around you, it seems that you're seeing an accurate representation of reality. However, these images have been subjected to all sorts of processes not only in the brain itself, but even in the eyes. You see, the eyes contain ten times as many light-sensitive cells as nerves that go back to the visual cortex. Therefore, in terms of data processing, ninety percent of the visual processing is actually done in your eyes. When the information finally reaches your visual cortex, it is processed further so that your brain can identify what you are looking at, where it is, what direction it is moving in, and how fast it is moving. And if you happen to be looking at a human face, your brain is processing even more to determine whose face you are looking at. What you actually see is your friend John walking toward you. All the massive amounts of visual processing that your eyes and your brain did are outside of your conscious attention; they are "unconscious" or "transparent," in the language of neuroscience.

However, when we talk about the True Unconscious in Tree of Life Coaching, we are not talking about raw data processing, even though it may be outside of conscious awareness (and therefore technically "unconscious"). That's why we don't simply referred to the unconscious mind—we refer to the *True Unconscious* to make it clear that we don't simply mean *any* unconscious mental process.

When we talk about the True Unconscious, we're talking about functions of the mind that guide your life—that cause you to make the decisions you make and engage in the behaviors you engage in. In particular, we are talking about your unconscious ability to track all your sensory experience, all your thoughts, and all your emotions, and to make sense and meaning of this extraordinary amount of information.

The True Unconscious is linked to every other branch of the Tree of Life (except the Real World because the Sensory Model of the World lies between). Therefore, there are essentially two aspects of this True Unconscious: the aspect that faces down toward the bottom of your Tree of Life, which we call the observing unconscious mind, and the aspect that faces up toward the top of the Tree of Life, which we call the orienting unconscious mind.

The Observing Unconscious Mind

Experience

Consciously you can only track seven, plus or minus two, pieces of information. This means you can only track between five and nine pieces of information, and more recent research indicates that this is a vast overestimation of the capability of your conscious mind! To experience this limitation, begin to pay attention to your left foot, now to your right foot, now to the sounds in the room around you, now to your left hand, now to your right hand, now to any smells around you in the room, now to something you can see on the other side of the room, now to whatever you can see out of the corner of your eye, now to the sounds outside of the room, and now, as you pay attention to the top of your head, you may well find that you are no longer aware of your left foot, at least until I mentioned it again!

However, your conscious mind is tracking everything at once. So if a fly landed on the back of your hand, you would immediately be aware of it because your unconscious mind draws it to your attention. Allow your awareness to "open up" to take in everything that your unconscious mind is aware of. Don't try and differentiate any specific sensation, such as "the feeling in my left foot"; rather, be aware of everything as a whole. Allow everything you feel, everything you see, everything you hear, everything you smell, and everything you taste to become part of one experience of the world around you. As you do so, become aware of the feelings inside your body (Emotion) and any sounds or pictures playing inside your mind (Thought).

The more you practice this exercise, the easier you'll find it. You will be able to open up to this vast band of information that your unconscious mind is tracking in each and every moment!

What Is the Observing Unconscious Mind?

The observing unconscious mind is the aspect of the True Unconscious that links down to the branches of Emotion, Thought, and the Sensory Model of the World. The observing unconscious mind is aware of every emotion you are feeling in your body, every thought you are thinking in your head (including your internal pictures and dialogue), and every piece of sensory information you are experiencing about the world around you through your eyes, ears, nose, skin, taste buds, and other sensory organs.

It's important to remember that you are not consciously aware of all this information (unless you make a conscious effort to become aware of it). You probably were not aware of the feeling of the clothes on your body until I mentioned it, and you may not have been aware of the sounds of the world around you until I mentioned them. But your observing unconscious mind is aware of all these things. This is why you pay attention whenever you hear somebody mention your name, even if you're not part of that conversation. Your unconscious mind was paying attention all along.

The Orienting Unconscious Mind

Experience

Choose one thing in the world around you. It can be an object, another person, a pet—whatever you want, as long as it's a real physical object.

Take a look at the object and begin to notice all the associations your brain is making. Perhaps you are thinking about all the times in the past when you used it, or the time when you bought it, or the person who gave it to you, or something else it reminds you of, or what you might do with it in the future. Taking in all these mental associations, ask yourself the question, "What does this object mean to me?"

If you come up with an answer, all well and good. If not, ask yourself a question that involves a decision such as "Should I throw this object away?" When forced to make a Real World decision, your unconscious mind will likely tell you exactly what the object means to you.

What Is the Orienting Unconscious Mind?

The orienting unconscious mind is the aspects of the True Unconscious that links sensory experience, thoughts, and emotions to the higher branches of the Tree of Life: Rules, Energy, Archetypes, Wisdom, and the Source. These links provide a framework within which your True Unconscious makes sense of the information gathered by the observing unconscious mind.

Comparing the Observing Unconscious and the Orienting Unconscious

Let's consider a quick example of how your observing unconscious mind interacts with your orienting unconscious mind. Suppose I am walking down the street and I see a man carrying a gun step out of the doorway in front of me. What should I do?

Well, first of all, my unconscious mind is going to decide whether the information is important based upon the context I'm in. If my unconscious mind decides that the information is not important, it likely won't even bring it to my conscious attention. For example, if I happen to be walking through a hunting town, or a military base, or even a movie studio, I might not pay too much attention to a man with a gun. If I'm walking through the streets of New York and the

204

man I see is dressed in a police uniform, again I'm not likely to pay too much attention to the fact that he's carrying a gun.

However, if I'm walking on the streets of New York and someone walks out of the building in front of me wearing street clothes and carrying a gun in his hand, I might have a very different reaction. My unconscious mind will likely grab the attention of my conscious mind and point out what is happening. Man with a gun! Bear in mind that we are not talking about what I think the man might be doing—we're talking about how I react in the first instant. So if the gun is contextually appropriate, for example, because it's being worn in a holster by a policeman, my body may stay relaxed. But if it is not contextually appropriate, my body may automatically go into a "fight or flight or freeze" mode. This is not about me thinking about the situation—the reaction is unconscious and immediate.

Having "observed" the gun, I now have to orient myself. This orientation will depend upon the higher-level branches on my Tree of Life: my beliefs, values, and archetypes. My orienting unconscious is linked to, and therefore aware of, all these higher aspects. Having called my conscious attention to the existence of the gun, I am going to orient my Tree of Life, rooted in this Real World experience, which will allow me to make a decision and take action.

Training the True Unconscious

Your unconscious mind is obviously not under the control of your conscious mind—that's why it's unconscious! The good news is that your True Unconscious—the part of you, your spirit, your soul, that truly wants the best for you—is capable of learning. It is also capable of drawing on the power of the Source, the power of the divine, the power of whatever principles are highest for you in the universe.

Using hypnosis or other trance experiences such as meditation, you can change the physical wiring in your brain and hence change your unconscious responses to external events. This, in turn, will change your emotional state on a long-term basis. For example, long-term meditation not only changes your emotional state as you meditate and immediately afterward; it also lowers your levels of anxiety and stress on a long-term basis. It can even increase the size and strength of the parts of your brain that give you emotional control.

Pathways

The True Unconscious is linked to every other branch of the Tree of Life with the exception of the Real World (to which it is linked indirectly through the Sensory Model of the World).

The True Unconscious tracks new information coming up from the lower branches (Thought, Emotion, and the Sensory Model of the World, and indirectly the Real World). This represents the flow of energy upward to the True Unconscious from lower branches.

Your True Unconscious then sends this information upward to higher branches, allowing them to orient to the new information. The higher branches send energy back down to the True Unconscious, laying out the meaning of the information and allowing the True Unconscious to orient to it.

Once the True Unconscious is oriented to the current Real World context, as well as to your thoughts and feelings about that context, your True Unconscious sends messages telling your brain what to think, your body what to feel, and your senses what to pay attention to. Your True Unconscious also tells your body how to move and react; Benjamin Libet's research demonstrated that all physical actions are controlled by the unconscious.

Your unconscious mind then tracks new information coming in from the context around you, and the cycle starts again.

Chapter 21: Rules – Gevurah - Power

We now come to the branch in the Tree of Life that represents Rules. You can think of these rules as specific types of belief about what you can and can't do, should and shouldn't do, must and mustn't do, and so on. These are essentially beliefs that control your movement through the world by either preventing you from doing something or making you do something, or sometimes making you feel guilty about doing or not doing it!

These types of beliefs can arise from your upbringing (perhaps what your parents told you should and shouldn't do), your religious or social culture ("don't steal," "don't eat with your mouth open," "tidy up after yourself"), or your experiences ("I can't dance—I've got two left feet").

The branch of Rules lies in the middle of the left-hand column of your Tree of Life (i.e., for your Tree of Life it lies on your left, but for your client's Tree of Life it lies on his or her left, therefore on your right as you're facing him or her).

Experience

Consider some area of your professional life where you haven't achieved as much as you would like. Step back into the last time and place you experienced that lack of achievement, see what you saw, and hear what you heard. Notice how you are feeling now…

As you are feeling this, ask yourself the question, "Why haven't I been able to achieve more?" If your mind responds with a reason that is based upon who you are or are not ("I'm just not good enough") or what you can't do ("I can't sell"), the problem lies in the branch of Rules.

Now consider some area of your professional life where you've been enormously successful. Step back into the last time and place you experienced that, see what you saw, and hear what you heard. Notice how you are feeling.

As you are feeling this, ask yourself the question, "How have I been able to achieve so much?" The answer may reveal a positive belief you hold about yourself in the branch of Rules ("I can do that—easily…").

Compare and contrast the beliefs that you identified in the two parts of this exercise. Repeating this exercise across a number of different contexts may reveal those beliefs that have had the greatest impact on your life.

Above Rules on the left-hand column lies the branch of Archetypes. The energy that flows through Archetypes flows straight down into the branch of Rules. Many of the beliefs that we hold come from the Archetypes that we model ourselves on, consciously or unconsciously. These Archetypes may be based on our parents, cultural icons (for example, movie stars or other celebrities), or religious teachings. Or we may more consciously model ourselves on individual Archetypes, such as a favorite teacher, and take our beliefs from them.

Below the branch of beliefs in the left-hand column lies the branch of Thought. Our beliefs give rise to our thoughts, so if you have a client who believes that he or she can't do something, the client probably say to him- or herself something like, "I can't do that." This thought arises from, but also gives life to, the belief.

Of course, the branch of Rules is connected to the branch of the True Unconscious. Negative beliefs can act through the unconscious mind to cause all sorts of problems, just as it is possible through the unconscious mind to create all sorts of healthy possibilities. The branch of Rules is also connected laterally to the branch of Energy, directly across on the right-hand column.

Meaning in Kabbalah

The branch of Rules is called Gevurah in the traditional Tree of Life, meaning Power. In Kabbalah, it is sometimes referred to as the "diamond cutter" because it gives shape to the energy of Chesed (Energy). Chesed is like an uncut diamond—it needs to be cut into facets to give it a useful form.

Let's consider a couple of metaphors to explain how this works. Consider an atomic power plant: if you simply begin an atomic reaction in the nuclear material, you are liable to end up with a nuclear explosion. Initial energy releases more atomic particles, which set up more reactions, which release even more particles, until the whole thing goes critical and explodes. In this metaphor, Gevurah represents the carbon rods that can be lowered into the core of the reactor to absorb the particles and control the amount of energy that is released so that it may be directed as electrical power into our homes, schools, and factories. In the same way, Rules limit the flow of energy from Chesed in some directions where we "mustn't," "shouldn't," or "can't" go so that our lives don't "go critical." And it directs energy in other directions where we "must," "should," or "can" go in order to power our lives.

Let's take a more human example: consider somebody who studies the martial arts. The person learns powerful techniques of kicking and punching that will allow him or her to direct his or her energy and potentially seriously hurt another person. This is why any reputable martial arts teacher will also teach philosophical tenets of the art that stress the responsible use of the techniques so that they are only used for self-defense. These tenets, or rules, are a manifestation of Gevurah, which controls and gives ethical and moral shape to the martial art.

Meaning in Tree of Life Coaching

When we say "beliefs" in the branch of Rules, we are referring to the rules that govern your individual world. Rules are absolute vital to living a balanced and harmonious life.

Of course, many of these rules may be shared with other people through your culture or religion. Many philosophical, religious, and spiritual systems stress one particular rule, which is stated as "treat others as you would have them treat you." This rule is deemed to be so important that it's often referred to as the Golden Rule. It appears in the philosophical moral systems of cultures as diverse as Babylonia, ancient China, Judaism, and Western philosophy.

So when we are talking about the branch of Rules, we not referring to beliefs such as the existence of God or other spiritual beliefs, which are better associated with the Source. And we are not talking about what you believe might be good for you; these beliefs are better associated with the Energy branch because they represent values. The beliefs in the branch of Rules are intended to place constraints on what you, personally, can and can't do. Unfortunately, sometimes we pick up beliefs or rules that limit us unnecessarily. For example, let's say you have a client (a man, for this example) who comes for coaching because he is not fulfilling his potential. He might be acting according to a set of beliefs such as:

- I can't do that.
- I'm not good enough.
- The world is not fair.

If he has such limiting beliefs, you as the coach will need to help him change these into more empowering beliefs.

On the other hand, he may have very positive beliefs about himself:

- I can do that—I can do anything!

- I'm the best!
- I'm going to conquer the world!

If he does have these types of beliefs, they may need to be tempered by a set of rules that tell him how to interact with other people. If he *only* has beliefs about his own amazing abilities, and lacks rules about how to treat other people, he may become arrogant and self-centered. A good example of this is arguably Steve Jobs, who had an amazingly positive set of beliefs about what was possible in the world and, in particular, what was possible for him. However, his rules about how to treat other people sometimes led him to have problems in his personal relationships. For example, for many years he refused to acknowledge his daughter because her birth had been inconvenient for him. While he was busy pursuing amazing possibilities in his business, he arguably lacked a healthy rule about how to treat members of his own family as well as friends and colleagues.

One of your responsibilities as a coach is to ensure that your client's life is governed by a set of healthy beliefs or rules: beliefs about the world, himself, and his place in the world as well as beliefs that empower him. And at the same time, he needs to have win-win rules that optimize his relationships with other people.

Coaching Example

You have a female client who comes to see you for weight loss. She tells you:

"I've always been overweight. My mother was overweight as well."

She is giving you two clues that she has a problem that lies in the Rules (beliefs) branch of the Tree of Life, triggered by an archetype (her mother). The first clue is that she has said "always." If she had instead said, "I'm overweight because I spent the holidays with my mother, and she makes me eat more than I should…" this would lie in the branch of her Sensory Model of the World because she would be saying, "My mother *causes* me to overeat." In contrast, beliefs from the branch of Rules generally extend to all times and all places, so you'll often hear words such as *always, everywhere,* and *everyone,* or alternatively, *never, nowhere,* and *no one.*

In fact, there is no such thing as "always"—especially in relation to weight. There are big babies, and there are small babies, but the doctor does not tell a new mother that her baby is "overweight." No one is overweight at birth.

The second clue is the reference by the client to her mother. The implication of this observation is that your client is overweight because her mother was overweight. At first, this may sound like a cause-and-effect in the branch of Sensory Model of the World: "My mother being overweight caused me to be overweight." However, if you think about it, this only makes sense if your client's mother is acting as an archetype for your client in the context of her weight: "I learned the Rules of being overweight from my mother."

It is going to be very difficult for your client to make changes in her behaviors that impact her weight (i.e., diet and exercise behaviors) or in how she feels about her weight as long as she holds this negative belief about her weight. Remember, energy tends to flow down the Tree of Life, in this case, down from the branch of Archetypes to the branch of Rules and from there to the lower triad of the Tree of Life.

Therefore, as a coach, one of your jobs is going to be to change her belief about herself and weight.

Pathways

When we consider the client's Tree of Life, there are four pathways that lead into the branch of Rules (beliefs) representing the four easiest and most direct ways to influence and ultimately change your client's beliefs. These pathways come from the branches of Archetypes, Energy, Thought, and the True Unconscious.

Archetypes Pathway

The pathway that leads from the branch of Archetypes to the branch of Rules can be used to positively impact beliefs by choosing a new archetype—one who holds empowering beliefs and empowering rules that can help your client to help herself, if she chooses to adopt them.

By the way, this is why companies that sell weight-loss programs will often use a celebrity spokesperson who has lost weight using that program—because that celebrity acts as an archetype for people using the product. This is true for men as well as women, which is why Weight Watchers uses spokespeople as diverse as Jessica Simpson and Charles Barkley. Most men could not imagine having Jessica Simpson as an archetype for themselves because she is a woman, but Charles Barkley, who is not only a man but also a great athlete, can be an excellent archetype for men seeking to lose weight.

If you want to learn more about using archetypes to make amazing changes in your life and the lives of your clients, please read our book *Deep Trance Identification*, by Shawn Carson and Jess Marion with John Overdurf, from Changing Mind Publishing, available at Amazon.com.

Energy Pathway

The Energy pathway can be used very effectively to change beliefs by encouraging your client to take up some energetic activity that inherently contains its own set of empowering beliefs. A good example of this is the traditional fire walk that is often done by Tony Robbins and other personal development gurus. Walking across fire brings with it a set of empowering beliefs along the lines of, "If I can walk on fire, I can do anything!!!"

Within a group environment, activities might be chosen that not only contain personally empowering beliefs, but also rules that govern how one person interacts with another. A great example of this in the corporate world is teambuilding retreats, in which a team of individuals is sent to an environment where they have to complete some physical or mental challenge, from solving team puzzles to climbing a mountain together as a team. These programs are designed to build positive and empowering individual beliefs through the successful completion of the challenge, and at the same time to give participants the opportunity to interact with their teammates according to a set of clear social rules that encourage group reliance and teamwork.

Thought Pathway

It goes without saying that energy flows down from the branch of Rules to the branch of Thought. If I believe something, I'm likely to consciously think it as well.

Perhaps the simplest way to change beliefs is using a pathway from thoughts. Thoughts can be controlled quickly and easily, and changing thoughts can begin to make changes in a client's underlying beliefs.

A quick and simple way to change beliefs is by using one of the belief change patterns from NLP. Using this pattern, the disempowering belief is represented as a picture in the client's mind's eye. The qualities (submodalities, in the jargon of NLP) of this picture, such as the size of the picture, the location of the picture, the distance of the picture, and so on, are noted. The submodalities are then changed into the submodalities of something that the client used to believe but doesn't believe anymore.

For example, let's say your female client has a belief, "I can't do this," and she sees a picture of herself failing at something. Suppose that picture is right in front of her and very close. Now if she thinks about something that used to be true for her but isn't anymore—for example, she used to have a red tricycle when she was a child—that picture is on the left-hand side and far away. All you do as the coach is to lead the client to take that first picture (the one of her failing) and move it off so that it is on the left-hand side and far away, exactly in the place where she kept that red tricycle—the "no longer true" location. Typically this would be done using a "slingshot" where the picture is first moved off into the distance and then moved back into the "used to be true" location.

A picture would then be made of the new belief, a picture in which the client is able to "do this," and that picture will be mapped across in the same way, but this time into the location of something that the client knows to be true. You can find this technique laid out in detail in any standard NLP textbook.

True Unconscious Pathway

The branch of Rules is also linked to the branch of the True Unconscious. Please refer to Chapter 20, on the True Unconscious, for a discussion of energy flow on this pathway.

Chapter 22: Energy – Chesed - Mercy

The Energy branch of the Tree of Life lies in the middle of the right-hand column (on your right side for your Tree of Life, or on your left for your client's Tree of Life as you face him or her). The Energy branch lies under the branch of Wisdom and over the branch of Emotion.

As well as being linked to Wisdom above it and the branch of Emotion below it, the Energy branch is also linked to the branch of Rules on the left-hand column and, of course, the True Unconscious.

Experience

Stand with your feet shoulder width apart with your hands by your sides. Check inside and notice how you feel. Pay particular attention to the feelings inside your body rather than trying to name your emotions. Does the energy *flow* up, or down, or does it move around in some other way?

Now think of some small problem—something that bothers you. Think perhaps of somebody you know who makes you feel irritated or angry. Or perhaps some event that makes you feel anxious. Whatever it is, pick something small. Think back to the last time you experienced that event, see what you saw, and hear what you heard. Now go back inside and check how you feel inside. How has the *flow* of energy changed?

Now blank that internal movie screen. Breathe in, and as you breathe in, raise your arms out to the sides to shoulder height, palms down. Continue breathing in and bend your elbows so your hands move toward the center of your chest, keeping your palms facing down. As you breathe out, begin to gently lower your hands down the center of your body as if pushing a weight down with the palms of your hands. Feel your own weight sinking into the ground. Repeat this for two more breaths (this exercise, from chi kung, is called "sinking the chi"). Notice the changes to the flow of energy inside your body as you do this.

Now think of your highest value—the thing that gets you up in the morning—and think back to the last time you fully experienced this, a time when you fully expressed this in your life. Go back to that time, see what you saw, and hear what you heard. Now check inside and notice how the *flow* of energy inside your body has changed.

Meaning in Kabbalah

In Kabbalah, Chesed represents the first Sephirot below the upper triad, meaning the first point of actual existence below the divine. Therefore, Chesed represents the point where the divine energy of the upper triad is manifest. It is not yet the physical manifestation of the physical body, and not even the flow of energy within that body at a specific time and place that we call *emotion*—it is rather more abstract than this.

Meaning in Tree of Life Coaching

In Tree of Life Coaching, the branch of Energy represents energy flows through your body. However, "energy" in this sense means your personal "subtle" energetic flow—your tendency to feel a certain way—rather than necessarily how you feel right now.

If you think of the higher points on the Tree of Life (the Source, Wisdom, and Archetypes), they are about the universe in general and so are very abstract. The Source represents the origin of the universe,

217

Wisdom represents differentiation into "this" and "that" or yin and yang, and Archetypes represents "idealized" forms of human beings. But the energy point is unique to you—it's very personal. You and I might both admire Steve Jobs as an archetype, but the energy that *you* feel based on the value you associate with Steve Jobs is different from the energy I feel based on the value I associate with Steve Jobs.

In Eastern philosophy, this type of energy is often called chi (or ki) energy. Chi energy represents the life force that governs your health, your movements, your digestion and internal organs—in fact, everything that makes you a living being. Chi energy is sometimes thought of as being breath and is circulated in the same way that the breath is circulated in the body.

In the coaching sense, we can also think of this energetic point as representing your values. By "values," I mean those values that shape your own personal destiny—perhaps your top one, two, or three values. A value in this sense is something that makes you feel good, and because we are talking about your top values, these are the things that make you feel alive. Perhaps for you these include freedom, or creativity, or love, but whatever they are, they should light you up inside like a flame. They should provide you with a passion to live your life as you choose. The branch of Energy represents the embodiment of the universal energy that has flowed down from the Source, through Wisdom and Archetypes, and into you as an individual.

Some people, especially those who practice some form of moving meditation, such as tai chi or yoga, or those who have experience in personal development through hypnosis or NLP, or those who practice somatic arts such as massage or Reiki, will find it very easy to pay attention to their own internal somatic experience, their own energy flows. Others, especially those who are not used to paying attention to their own body, may find it more difficult at first.

Paying attention to the flow of energy within your body is key to making a connection with universal energy. When you pay attention to this type of internal energy, it will tell you if you're moving in the right direction. Think of all the times when something didn't work out for you and when you look back on the decision that took you there, you just had a gut feeling that it was the wrong thing to do. Now think of all the times when you were in a peak state, you felt that flow of energy inside that let you know you could do anything, and you will see how much you achieved when you had that feeling. As Richard Bandler, cofounder of NLP, often says, you should pay attention to what makes you feel good. He doesn't mean this in a hedonistic way; rather, he means pay attention to the good feelings because these let you know what's really important to you.

Coaching Example

When you have a coaching client who "always" seems to be in one particular state—perhaps he or she is always angry or always "on top of the world"—this is a reflection of the client's Energy branch. Obviously, there is no such thing as "always" being in one state, so what I'm really talking about is someone who spends an unreasonable amount of time in a particular state. When a client spends much of his or her time in a state he or she does not enjoy, or a state that doesn't serve him or her well, the answer may be for the client to develop more options in his or her Energy branch.

A good example of this is when somebody becomes obsessed by an old relationship. This relationship may come to "'possess" the client; perhaps he or she is always angry or simply hopes against hope that he or she will win back the old partner. This arises from a "lover archetype" that the client no longer has access to, and the "lack" of that person flows down into the branch of Energy.

Of course, if your client "always" feels fantastic, he or she is probably moving in the right direction! At the same time, there is nothing wrong with being a serious person, any more than there's anything wrong with being a jovial person. I remember an episode of the original *Star Trek* series where Dr. McCoy says to Mr. Spock, "You're the most cold-blooded man I know!" to which Spock replies, "Why, thank you, Doctor."

The question is whether your branch of Energy serves you as you want it to. If it does, fine. If not, you can take steps to change your energy, and in changing your energy, change your dominant emotional states.

The most direct way to work on your Energy branch is to engage in some activity specifically designed to change your energy over the long-term, like tai chi, chi kung, yoga, or other energy exercises that involve some type of moving meditation or breathwork. Even a daily walk in nature can be sufficient to develop and invigorate your Energy branch.

You can also surround yourself with appropriate archetypes for the energy you want to develop. I have already mentioned Norman Cousins. Cousins was diagnosed with cancer and treated himself by watching comedy films. As he tells the story, surrounding himself with these archetypes of laughter shifted his energy, and therefore the emotions he felt most of the time, to laughter, and his cancer was healed.

Values in the Branch of Energy

As mentioned above, one way to think of the branch of Energy, especially within the context of coaching, is as the location where we keep our values. In the coaching context, we can define a value as a word that leads to a positive emotion; for example, whenever I say the word *freedom* I feel good.

Obviously there's a lot more to freedom than this. For example I have my own ideas about what freedom represents (in the branch of Thoughts), powerful memories of times when I actually felt free (in the branch of Archetypes), a desire to respect the freedom of others (in the branch of Rules), and so on. But values themselves lie in the branch of Energy.

A popular tool in any coach's tool kit is to discover your client's highest values. If you can do this, you can immediately "light up" your client's branch of Energy simply by mentioning his or her highest values. If the client has come to you because he or she wants to feel a certain way, or engage in a certain behavior, he or she can be primed to do so if that feeling or that behavior is linked to his or her highest values. One easy way to do this is to ask your client how he or she is expressing his or her highest value when engaged in that activity. For example, if your client's highest value is freedom, and he or she wanted to finish writing his or her first book, you might say something like:

"As you are finishing your book, how are you living free (or "being free")?"

You can then feed back to your client whatever he or she says to you to begin to link, or anchor, the value of freedom with the writing of his or her book.

Pathways

As we discussed above, pathways lead to the Energy branch from the branches of Wisdom, Rules, the True Unconscious, and Emotion.

The Pathway from Wisdom to the Branch of Energy

In order to draw energy from Wisdom, the place of potential, you have to ask yourself, or ask your client:

"Aside from anything you felt in your life so far, what's everything else you could be feeling right now, that is really important to you, now?"

Using the spatial preposition "aside from" allows something new to develop, and using the creative induction of "everything else" will take your client to Wisdom. Finally, asking "that is really important to you" directs the client's attention down from Wisdom into the branch of Energy (i.e., values).

When you begin to ask these types of questions with a sense of expectation, you will find that an answer comes to your client (or to you). And when the answer comes to you, you will begin to feel that way.

The Pathway from the Branch of Rules to the Branch of Energy

For some people, particularly if it is part of their cultural and social upbringing, the branch of Rules can directly influence the branch of Energy. For example, think of the "stiff upper lip" that was expected of the British aristocracy in Victorian times. If you were born into the British aristocracy, you were expected at all times to maintain a state of calm and reserve, no matter what was going on around you. This has been true of many cultures around the world over many centuries. For example, samurai warriors would stoically choose to commit ritual suicide following any perceived stain on their honor.

In the modern world, especially in Western culture, displays of a wide range of emotions are quite acceptable, compared to some other cultures where emotional dsiplays are socially 'taboo'. I have a male friend who bursts into tears whenever he reads a play or novel out loud, another friend who breaks into giants guffaws of laughter at the slightest provocation, and an acquaintance who seems to spend his life yelling obscenities into the phone because he is angry about one thing or another. Because our modern rules allow such a wide range of emotional response, there is more freedom to find your own range within your branch of Energy. The branch of Rules, therefore, has less control over the branch of Energy because everything is "allowed."

The Pathway from the True Unconscious to the Branch of Energy

Any type of trance work, self-hypnosis, or meditation practiced on a long-term basis can lead to changes in the client's Energy branch. A great example of this is gratitude meditation, or compassion meditation. A number of research studies indicate that compassion, including self-compassion, is one of the most powerful emotional tools to do this.

For example, if you want to practice compassion meditation, a good way of doing so is to:

- First think about somebody you love and feel a sense of compassion for that person. Spend some time really getting in touch with that sense of compassion for him or her. That should be fairly easy.

- Now think about somebody you know whom you feel neutral about—perhaps a neighbor or somebody you work with. Spend some time and meditate until you get in touch with a sense of compassion for him or her as well.

- Now think of somebody who's a stranger—perhaps you've seen the person serving in a coffee shop but have never really spoken to him or her. Meditate on the person until you begin to feel a sense of compassion for him or her as well.

- Now think of somebody you don't like—your enemy. Spend some time thinking of that person until you can feel compassion for him or her as well.

- Finally, think about yourself and feel compassion for yourself.

If you carry out the above exercise on a regular basis, you will experience powerful shifts in your Energy branch—shifts that will allow you to feel compassion for the whole world.

The Pathway from the Branch of Emotion to the Branch of Energy

The pathway from the branch of Emotion to the branch of Energy can be used to change your energy in a particular context. If you want to feel a different emotion in a specific context, all you have to do is "anchor" that emotion to that context.

For example, if you are coaching somebody who wants to feel more confident in public speaking, all you have to do is lead that person into a sense of confidence and attach it to the context of public speaking. Ask your client to think about an activity he or she does that makes him or her feel confident, and as he or she is feeling that, to picture the eyes of the audience on him or her.

If you generalize this out by asking your client to think about lots of contexts where he or she might be speaking in public—for example, presentations at work, making speeches at a social occasion, or simply telling a joke to friends—that sense of confidence will be available to him or her across a wider set of contexts. Ultimately, this sense of confidence becomes part of your client's "everyday" repertoire of emotional responses. In other words, it becomes part of his or her Energy branch in the Tree of Life.

Chapter 23: Archetypes – Binah – Understanding

The top portion of the Tree of Life is made up of three points that form another triangle, or triad, but this time they are pointing upward. Each branch in this upper triad represents ideas that are greater than the individual him- or herself and are therefore also more abstract. This is in contrast to the lower two triads, which represent ideas that are specific to the individual whose Tree of Life it is.

The top point of this upper triad is the Source of universal energy, the next branch being Wisdom representing the creative potential, and the third branch is the branch of Archetypes. The branch of Archetypes lies on the left-hand column of your Tree of Life (on the left for you, and therefore your client's branch of Archetypes lives on your right as you look at your client).

Archetypes represent the point where the potential of the universe is manifested in an exemplar such as a person or event representing the best (or worst) of humanity. The branch of Archetypes represents *your* archetypal representation of a person, object, event, or concept. For example, you might watch a touchdown being scored and say something like, "Now, that was teamwork!" That one particular touchdown would be an archetypal representation of "teamwork" for you. Or you may have seen those posters showing a motivational photograph together with a word or short phrase, for example, a picture of a rowing team with the word *Teamwork* above it—an archetypal representation for the designer of the photograph.

Of course, an archetypal representation will often be a person. Perhaps you think of Albert Einstein as representing genius, or Steve Jobs as representing creativity. Stepping into this archetype will allow you to take on that person's Tree of Life.

Experience

Spend a few moments to come up with an archetypal memory or representation of the following:

- Now that's teamwork!
- Now that's genius!
- Now that's comedy!
- Now that's determination!
- Now that's confidence!
- Now that's creativity!
- Now that's courage!
- Now that's skill!

Archetypes and Aristotle's Forms

The Greek philosopher Aristotle, who called these archetypes "forms," originally developed this idea of archetypes. He gave the example of the idea of a horse; if I ask one hundred people to think of a horse, they will all think of a horse, but the horse will be different for each person. For example, one person might think of a white horse in a field, another might think of a brown horse been ridden by a cowboy, a third might think of a black horse pulling a cart, while a fourth might think of a bucking bronco. The idea of "horse" is common to all of these representations, so "horse" represents the form. At the same time, there are many examples of specific horses. Indeed, outside of mathematics, it's impossible to think of a pure "form" without thinking of a specific representation of that form. It's impossible to think of the form "horse" without bringing to mind a specific horse from a specific context. But on some level, the specific horse you bring to mind represents "horses" in general, as a class of animal. Whichever horse you specifically think of represents an archetype for you.

So an archetype is a person, object, event, or memory that is *representative* of a general class or concept.

Meaning in Kabbalah

In the Kabbalah, this point is known as Binah, which means understanding. Binah turns the abstract into a practical skill. Binah is sometimes represented as the birth canal through which the unlimited potential of the Source and Void are compressed into something on a more human scale.

Meaning in Tree of Life Coaching

The point of Archetypes has two main meanings or applications in Tree of Life Coaching:

Memories as Archetypes

Probably the most important aspect of the branch of Archetypes is the use of memory. The reason we, as human beings, have such wonderful memories is that our memories act as sources of wisdom or knowledge, telling us what to do in specific contexts. As we evolved into humans, we faced a number of threats to our existence from wild animals, floods, fires, other natural disasters, poisoned food, competing tribes, and many other existential situations.

Our distant ancestors reacted to these threats and survived, while other potential humans reacted in different ways and did not survive. Darwinian evolution meant that whatever reaction worked was encoded in the DNA of the descendants of the successful human prototypes. However, the survival of the fittest as encoded in DNA was not sufficient for human beings to fulfill their destiny as children of God. Each individual human being is precious and therefore learns to encode his or her own experiences not just in DNA through gene expression (which, incidentally, can also be passed on to future generations), but also as memories that could guide the future behavior of that individual.

When choosing which memories to use as reference experiences, your unconscious mind will select those from situations that were "similar" to the situation you find yourself in now. "Similar" in this context may mean in the same or a similar place, or when you were feeling the same emotion, or even when you were smelling a similar smell.

It's not surprising that your unconscious mind selects behaviors from similar situations you have experienced in the past that are found in your memories. After all, if those behaviors allowed you to survive in the past, your unconscious mind knows that they work as far as survival is concerned! Unfortunately, this means that your unconscious mind tends to repeat behaviors, even behaviors that didn't work very well the first time. This is particularly true when you are under stress because under stress, your "executive" brain tends to give over control to your unconscious instinctive mind.

So, for example, if you have a client (say a male) who has a fear of public speaking and he has to give a speech, he will become stressed. When he becomes stressed, his behaviors are likely to be selected by his unconscious mind on the basis of whatever allowed him to "survive" in the past. This applies even if that past event involved a week of sleepless nights prior to the speech! In order to help clients like this one, you must provide them with a new archetypal response.

Archetypes as Archetypes

The other, and perhaps more obvious, meaning for the branch of Archetypes is as a source of archetypal wisdom. For example, if you want to become more creative, perhaps you should model Steve Jobs, perhaps Leonardo da Vinci or Georgia O'Keeffe. These historical individuals can act as archetypes for the creativity you are seeking.

Each of these archetypes has his or her own Tree of Life. Actually, they have many Trees, one for every significant event in their life, but their "creative" Trees in particular can act as archetypes for your own creativity or that of your clients. By exploring the life events of these archetypes, you and your clients can discover, and try on, the Tree of Life they were experiencing during that event.

Experience

Think about a situation in which you would like to respond differently—more resourcefully—than you usually do.

Think about somebody—an archetype—you know (or know of) who would respond in this resourceful way to the situation. Imagine you are watching that person on a movie screen in the situation, seeing him or her respond in this resourceful way. Imagine you are the film editor who is editing the movie until it's just the way you would like it to be. Run the movie as many times as you need to until it's perfect.

Now realize that you can use this as an archetype for your own responses. Simply imagine floating into the movie, floating into this archetype, and trying on this response for yourself.

As you do so, begin to explore the Tree of Life that you find yourself inside (the archetype's Tree of Life):

- How are you behaving as this archetype?
- What do you consider to be "causes" and "effects," and "meanings" as the archetype in this context?
- What are you thinking? What are you saying to yourself as the archetype? What pictures or movies are you seeing in your mind as this archetype?
- What emotions are you feeling in your body as the archetype?
- What is possible for you, or impossible for you, as the archetype in this context? What can you do and what can you not do? What should you do and what must you do?

- What is important to you as the archetype in this time and place?

When you have explored each of these questions, float out of the movie. Before you float back into yourself, consider what experiences and learnings you wish to take back with you and which ones you wish to leave behind.

When you're ready, float back into yourself.

Coaching Example

The archetypal experiences that often have the most impact on your client are those that took place in your client's childhood. Childhood years are formative. Early experiences, especially emotionally charged experiences, will immediately begin to shape our later reactions to similar circumstances. These formative experiences can very rapidly become the norm for all behaviors.

For example, if someone (a man, for this example) is a relatively competent public speaker and has to give a presentation at work, and his boss gives him some negative feedback about it, he may shrug it off or use that feedback to improve his presentations in the future. However, if a small child is giving a "presentation" at school in show-and-tell, and his classmates laugh at him or his teacher says he messed up, based on his embarrassment he could quickly generalize that to believing that he can't present or speak in public. This may cause him to feel stressed the next time he has to speak in front of the class, meaning he'll be even less likely to succeed, which strengthens the negative belief and increases the stress for the next time. It all becomes a negative, self-fulfilling prophecy.

One way to address these early archetypes with your coaching client is using a "reimprinting." Reimprinting is a technique that takes your client back to childhood, typically in a dissociated way so he can watch the events unfold from a distance without experiencing the negative feelings associated with the event. While he is watching the old events, he can "gift" resources to his younger self so that younger self is able to deal more resourcefully with the situation.

Please note that you should be very careful in doing reimprinting techniques unless you're properly trained. This is especially true if you're dealing with a client who experienced traumatic events in his or her childhood.

When the client remembers a situation in a new way, after he gifts resources to a younger version of himself in a situation in which he originally felt unresourceful, those resources become part of the memory. This is a process neuroscientists refer to as "memory reconsolidation." After the reimprinting, each time your client recalls that memory in the future, it will also contain these new resources. The memory will cease to be a negative archetypal experience and may even become a positive archetypal memory for him.

Pathways

The branch of Archetypes has four pathways connecting it to other branches of the Tree of Life—to the Source, Wisdom, Rules, and the True Unconscious.

The pathway that leads from the Source to Archetypes is often activated when the universe creates some unexpected opportunity or other event that changes everything. A new baby may transform a career-driven executive into a doting mother. A sudden parental illness may transform a selfish son into a compassionate caregiver. The archetype is essentially chosen by the universe and imposed on the individual.

And sometimes a person will be born as, or transformed into, an individual who is so archetypal that he or she changes the universe. This may be a Steve Jobs, Rosa Parks, Albert Einstein, Mother Teresa, or Gandhi. On the dark side, it might be an Adolf Hitler.

The pathway that runs from Wisdom to Archetypes creates physical expression of a new thought, a new paradigm that arises out of Wisdom. Tony Robbins activates this pathway when he asks his clients the question, "If you wake up tomorrow and anything is possible, who will you be?"

As always, the True Unconscious looks upward to the branches of Rules, Energy, Archetypes, Wisdom, and the Source to orient itself to the current context defined by the lower triad. Most of our orientation occurs unconsciously. Only a tiny portion is processed through Thought and is therefore accessible to the conscious mind. The archetypes provided by memories, and by archetypal figures we have known such as parents, are used in this orientation.

As a coach, one of your responsibilities is to help your client release as many negative archetypes (memories and archetypes that are not serving him or her well) and to replace them with positive archetypes that will serve him or her better. You can do this through reimprinting or through techniques such as Perfect Peace from EFT. You can also begin to build a more positive archetype in the future simply by focusing on the positive, for example, by keeping a "gratitude journal."

Within a coaching session, the pathway from Rules to Archetypes is very often triggered when your client explains the beliefs he or she holds that define the rules in his or her life—things like "I can't," "I shouldn't," "I have to," and so on. In order to explore these rules more deeply, you, as the coach, can simply ask, "Who taught you that?... Who told you that that was true?... And how old were you then?..." This is likely to take your client back to a memory, perhaps very early in life, when he or she was told that he or she couldn't, shouldn't, or had to. These memories can then be transformed using reimprinting.

Chapter 24: The Void – Hokhmah – Wisdom

Wisdom lies at the very top of your right-hand column (once again, Wisdom in your client's Tree of Life will be on your client's right, or your left as you look at your client). Being on the right-hand column, it lies above the branch of Energy, which in turn lies above the branch of Emotion. Therefore, Wisdom is a branch associated with somatic energy—energy inside the body. However, in the case of Wisdom, the feeling is one of uncertainty, even confusion.

Experience

This is a variation of an exercise developed by John Overdurf. Simply ask yourself each question and give yourself a few moments to fully and deeply consider it. Please realize that these questions are designed for your unconscious mind, and there are no "right" or "wrong" answers. In fact, you don't need to answer any of the questions at all— you just need to deeply consider them:

- Who are you, now?
- Where are you, now?
- When are you, now?
- Who wouldn't you be, if you weren't you?
- Where wouldn't you be, if you weren't here?
- When wouldn't you be, if you weren't now?
- Who are you, when you're any time but now?

- Who are you, when you're everywhere but here?
- Who are you now?

If you began to feel a sense of dislocation as you consider the above questions, that's perfectly normal!

Meaning in Kabbalah

In the Kabbalah, this branch—Wisdom—is called Hokhmah, meaning wisdom. In the Jewish Kabbalah, it represents creative energy, or creative potential, or infinite expansion.

Meaning in Tree of Life Coaching

The meaning of Wisdom in Tree of Life Coaching is the place where creative energy can be found. So, for example, if you have a new thought, a new idea, or a new energy, it arises from Wisdom. By creativity, I mean a new way of looking at things, a new paradigm.

Now, when you go to Wisdom, you go into a trance—sometimes a mini-trance yet nevertheless a trance. If you have ever asked somebody a question that he or she wasn't expecting, a question that came out of left field, you might see him or her go into a momentary state of confusion. Perhaps the person's eyes widened, or he or she looked up with his or her eyes moving from side to side while searching for an answer that wasn't immediately there. These are signs of trance.

You may also have experienced this on the receiving end. Somebody asks you a question and you go into a state in which your brain just seems to blank. It may only last a few seconds, and then you find your feet again—you find something to hold onto, and your brain starts to process again. But in those few seconds of mild confusion, you experience Wisdom.

We have a saying in HNLP that the conscious mind has no business choosing the state that you should be in at any time. This may be an overstatement, but what it means is that all too often when someone, say, a female client, is not feeling as resourceful as she would like, her conscious mind thinks, "I wish I didn't feel this way." When asked how she would like to feel instead, she either tells you what she doesn't want to feel, or she responds, "I'd rather feel…" and then fills in the blank with the exact opposite of what she's feeling at the moment. So if she's feeling nervous, she says she wants to feel confident, or if she feels agitated, she says she wants to feel calm. This is because the conscious mind likes to view the world through a prism of "black and white," in which there are only two emotional states or feelings: what you're feeling now, and the opposite of what you're feeling now. Because the conscious mind tends to process along these either-or spectrums of opposites, your client may miss out on the full spectrum of possible emotions and feelings.

In contrast, if you allow the unconscious mind to select the appropriate emotional state from the full universe of possibilities, the unconscious mind may choose something more appropriate. Of course, you have to bear in mind that the unconscious mind chose the stated problem in the first place! So the unconscious mind is not infallible. The unconscious mind therefore needs to be guided away from choosing the problem and toward the client's highest good.

The Two Magic Ingredients

There are two magic ingredients for leading a client into Wisdom. The first of these is to use negation—words like *not*, *but*, and *except*. Negation tells the unconscious mind to go anywhere except where it is right now. This is important because generally in coaching, "right here, right now" is where the problem is. The solution is somewhere else. Obviously, this does not apply if your client is already in a positive state!!!

So when your client tells you, "I want to feel anything except what I'm feeling right now," she is telling you that she lacks ("want" literally means a lack of) the ability to feel anything other than what she feels right now. It's no wonder she gets stuck!

235

To get your client unstuck, you need to "reboot" her brain, which involves a brief visit to Wisdom. When you ask your client something like, "What have you not been feeling that's everything except what you're feeling now?" you're posing a question for which she can't find an answer using her conscious mind. After all, the question really doesn't make an awful lot of sense on a conscious level!

Now, negation does not offer guidance as to how to get to anywhere or how to find an answer, because "there" is anywhere but here. So your client probably can't find the answer immediately using her conscious mind (because if she could, she wouldn't still be stuck in the problem). So what does she do? She goes into Wisdom to look for the answer.

I've already unconsciously shown you the second magic ingredient (remember, negation is the first), so let's just lay it out there for your conscious mind. The second magic ingredient is to ask your client a question that includes the word *everything*. When you ask for "everything," you are asking your client's brain to do the impossible. It is impossible for a human's conscious mind to think of "everything," because everything is just too big. Our conscious mind likes to have specific ideas—things it can count. Our conscious mind likes lists, preferably numbered lists. Our conscious mind doesn't handle "everything" very well!

Surprisingly, the same is true of the word *nothing*. "Nothing" is so difficult for the conscious mind to process that it took many centuries for mathematicians to invent the number zero! "Anything" can have a similar effect.

Because your conscious mind doesn't deal very well with the concept of 'everything', (or nothing or anything), it tends to hand these questions over to your unconscious mind to deal with. If it's easier to understand, you can substitute "your 'right -brain'" for the unconscious mind and "left -brain" for the conscious mind.

Thinking about "everything" (or anything or nothing) generates what is known as an "inductive" thought, meaning it forces you to search outward, expansively. By the way, the opposite of "induction" is "deduction," which involves choosing or discovering something specific.

Combining these two magic ingredients, negation and induction, stimulates the unconscious mind to search for something different from what's happening now (because we're using negation) by entering Wisdom (because we're using induction).

Coming Out of Wisdom

As I explained above, Wisdom is a type of trance. It's a trance of mild confusion. It's not a great idea to leave your client in Wisdom for too long, because she will remain confused. You want her to emerge from Wisdom, but to emerge in a resourceful place, creating a new Tree of Life as she does. You want this new Tree of Life to be as resourceful as possible.

The easiest way to do this is to leverage the power of values. Values lie on the branch of Energy, which, like Wisdom, is on the right-hand column of the Tree of Life. In fact, Energy lies immediately below Wisdom, so it's a really easy landing place for your client's mind when she emerges from Wisdom.

To leverage the power of values, you might want to say to your client something like, "What is really important to you now?" Of course, you had just asked her another question to throw her into Wisdom, so now you have a sequence of two questions:

"What's everything (induction) else but (negation) that?"

And…

"What's really important to you now?"

237

Because you only need her to remain in Wisdom for a few seconds, to reset her unconscious mind, you can simply ask these two questions within a single sentence, something like:

"What is everything else, that is anything but... that... is really important to you now?"

You'll notice that in this example, you have made the word *that* serve double duty, meaning it acts as the last word of the first sentence indicating the problem, and it also acts as the first word of the second sentence. This language pattern is called a "punctuational ambiguity," meaning that it's unclear where one sentence ends and another one begins.

This type of language is the basis of the type of coaching called attention shifting coaching, which was developed by John Overdurf. Attention shifting coaching was taken by Igor Ledichowski, who created his own coaching system known as Mind Bending Language. A full discussion of these systems is outside the scope of this book. However, if you simply know a few of the basic patterns, they will take you a long way.

Pathways to and from Wisdom

The branch of Wisdom has four pathways leading to and from other branches. These branches are the Source, Archetypes, Energy, and the True Unconscious.

The pathway from the Source to Wisdom is easy to understand within the context of a personal Tree of Life. The universe throws energy in my direction—perhaps I win the lottery, or perhaps I get fired from my job. Either way, the energy begins to flow down the Tree of Life and reaches Wisdom. The Void is the place of differentiation, where we make distinctions between one thing and another, where we make choices. So as this energy reaches Wisdom, I'm forced to decide what it means; on a very basic level, I have to decide whether this is a good thing or a bad thing.

Energy can also flow from Wisdom to the Source, meaning that if we make a new decision—a new distinction about how we view the world—it will tend to stimulate the universe to manifest according to this new distinction. This is often called "the Secret" (after the book of the same name).

The next pathway goes from Wisdom to the branch of Archetypes. Once we have made a decision or distinction or chosen a meaning in Wisdom (and hopefully stimulated the universe to release energy to manifest that distinction), we now have to take action. We have to decide what and how to think about this, how to feel about it, and so on. By choosing an archetype, which carries with it its own Tree of Life, our unconscious mind is able to populate this new Tree of Life according to this new distinction.

The third pathway goes from Wisdom to the branch of Energy. I've already talked about this pathway and how values, which arise in the branch of Energy, attract certain distinctions in Wisdom. Just to be clear what we're talking about, if you have a client whose problem is fear and whose most important value is "freedom," and you ask him or her:

"Aside from fear (negating the problem), what's everything else (inductive language pattern to take the client into Wisdom) that you're really free (using the client's value) to feel now?"

... then the feeling he or she picks will likely be one that is aligned with "freedom."

The final pathway, as usual, leads to the True Unconscious. The unconscious mind has direct access to Wisdom. As we have seen, the unconscious mind tends to access Wisdom whenever it comes across a question without a clear answer based in current or past experience.

Chapter 25: The Source – Kether – The Crown

At the very top of the Tree of Life lies the branch I have been calling the Source. The Source represents the energy provided by the universe, for example, in the form of random events. Bear in mind that strictly speaking, the energy that comes from the Source is neither good nor bad—it simply is. Judgment of this energy, including whether it is good or bad, initially takes place in Wisdom.

The Source is the highest point on the Tree of Life. It provides the energy for all the other points on the Tree.

The Source can be studied in many ways—through science, religion, spirituality, or simply through your own identity as a human being. I will move between these various descriptions in the course of this chapter. If you personally hold a specific worldview that accepts one description but not another, please feel free to ignore those parts that do not fit with your worldview. Life is a jewel with many facets, and you can choose to look at whichever of those facets you choose.

Scientifically, the Source represents the Big Bang, the start of the universe, the beginning of the expansion of time and space. The Source—the Big Bang—leads to the coalescing of energy into matter, and matter into stars, which over time exploded, releasing atoms such as carbon that form your body. You are literally a starchild.

Religiously, in the Judeo-Christian tradition, the Source represents Creation, when God breathed life into the universe as we know it. Other world religions have their own creation stories, and the Source can be thought of as the origin of these as well.

In the humanistic framework, for example, in your own life, you can think of the Source as being your own moment of conception. It is a moment in time when the blind watchmaker set your own personal timepiece in motion. It is this timepiece that will tick off the moments of your life and provide you with the time to create your own personal triumphs and disasters, dreams and calamities.

In its purest form, the energy of the Source can create extraordinary lives—the lives of extraordinary human beings who are driven by one pure energy—perhaps creativity, physical perfection, or the pursuit of power. The flow of this energy is so irresistible that it essentially forces individual humans to dedicate their lives to one task, to one idea. These human beings may become artists, composers, teachers, inventors, or athletes. In any case, they become vessels through which the energy of the Source flows.

In a sense, there is only one unique moment of conception for everything you are and everything you could be. Further, in a fatalistic view of the universe, once your timepiece has begun to tick, every moment of your life is predetermined. Miss that instant of infinite possibility, and you may be fated to live a life of mediocrity!

But there's another alternative, another view, that provides the rationale for studying the Tree of Life in the first place. This view says that it's possible to return to the Source, to begin again with unlimited human possibilities, to see the face of God through prayer or spiritual meditation, or to read the thoughts of God through the study of science. On its highest level, studying the Tree of Life seeks to take us back to the Source.

There are several different ways to experience the Source using exercises from hypnosis or NLP. For example, if you've ever experienced the NLP "drop-through" pattern (which you can find described in Brandon Hayes's book *The Journey*), you may have had an experience of visiting the Source when you "dropped through" the final emotion. This version of the Source is very often experienced as a dark, peaceful place where you feel at one with the universe. If you haven't experienced the drop-through, it provides a way to access deeper and deeper states by "dropping through" whatever emotion you're feeling at the time to discover what's underneath.

Another way of potentially accessing the Source, which in some ways is very similar to the drop-through, although in other ways is very different, is to use a series of inductive language questions. For example, if I were to ask you the question "Who are you?" you might answer by giving me your name, say, Jo. I might then ask you, "What's everything else you are, that's even more than simply being Jo?" And you might answer, "I'm a teacher" or whatever your profession is. And then I might ask, "What's everything else you are that's even more than simply being Jo and a teacher?" And each time you answer, I add what you just said to my definition of you and ask you for even more. Playing this game can lead to a feeling of expansion and ultimately a feeling of oneness with the universe!

Finally, those who are experienced meditators may also find Wisdom waiting for them in meditation.

Meaning in Kabbalah

In the Kabbalah, this point is called Kether, meaning the crown. It's the place of undifferentiated, pure energy. It can be thought of as God, or the manifestation of God in the universe, or in scientific terms, the Big Bang.

Meaning in Tree of Life Coaching

The meaning of this point, the Source, in Tree of Life coaching will very much depend on the client's beliefs. For some clients this point will indeed represent god or the divine. For others it may represent a more spiritual 'universal energy'. For those clients without a religious or spiritual viewpoint it will represent the hand or fate, or chance.

In any case it represents events that are outside the client's control, and yet that transform the client's life.

Experience

Spend a moment and consider what the highest source of wisdom is for you. This may not be the Source in the sense we are discussing in this chapter, so simply consider the teacher or the principles that you consider sacrosanct. It may be God, it maybe science. It may be the human spirit, or unlimited human potential. Or it may be a teacher, a rabbi, a priest, a guru, a Buddha. If it is a person, that person may be living, or he or she may be communicating with you via sacred writings, or through the pages of the *New York Times*.

If the highest source of wisdom for you is another human being or a book written by a human being, consider the source of *that person's* wisdom. If he or she learned from his or her own teacher, what is the source of *that* teacher's wisdom? Trace that chain of wisdom back as far as you can, from teacher to teacher. When you consider the influences that impacted each of the people in your lineage, you will come closer to the true Source.

In many systems of wisdom, and in HNLP, we call this chain of teachers a lineage. A lineage is a chain of wisdom, from teacher to student, that results in your own wisdom. The lineage is rarely linear, and you may be able to trace many paths back from where you are now to the Source of your wisdom.

After you have considered the source of your own wisdom and the lineage that led to that wisdom, consider how that wisdom is manifested in your life. Which of your behaviors arise from that particular wisdom? Which of your behaviors are consistent with that wisdom? And which of your behaviors violate that wisdom in some way?

Pathways

In the Tree of Life, the Source is connected to three other points:

- The Void
- Archetypes
- The True Unconscious

As mentioned above, the Source represents the energy of the Big Bang. At that point, space-time was so compressed, and matter and energy so densely packed, that there was essentially no differentiation as we understand it. Even the laws of physics as we understand them cannot be applied to this moment in time, because it is what physics calls a "singularity."

In the moments following the Big Bang, time and space began to expand. This expansion allowed the energy created by the Big Bang in space to coalesce into matter. It was this expansion of space-time, and the coalescence of energy, that allowed the matter to form so that we could distinguish a particle from the empty space around it. Ultimately this coalescence of energy into matter created, every star, every planet, every plant and animal, and every human being in the universe.

In more religious or spiritual terms, when we talk about the Source, we are talking about the mind of God. In this sense, at the moment of all creation, the mind of God has not yet differentiated between light and darkness, being and nonbeing, male and female, yin and yang. There is only light. It is said that God created the universe, and created human beings within the universe, in order to experience in the way that we experience, to be able to differentiate between one thing and

244

another. This differentiation originates at the next branch of the Tree of Life, in Wisdom.

So the Source represents undifferentiated energy. It is the pathway from the Source to Wisdom that allows differentiation between one thing and another.

Exercise

Read these instructions before you begin the exercise.

Close your eyes and completely blank your mind. For most people, this is impossible; no matter how hard we try to blank our minds, stray thoughts will enter in to fill the blank.

So this time, close your eyes and blank your mind, but then wait for the first thought to appear. Think of that thought and the opposite of that thought. So if the thought that creeps in is "black," think about black and think about white. It doesn't really matter what opposite you choose—just think about the thought and its opposite.

Now, close your eyes and blank your mind, and wait for the first thought to appear once more. This time, think of that thought, and also think of *anything* other than thought. So if the thought is "egg," think of egg and think of anything other than egg—maybe the Eiffel Tower.

One more time, close your eyes and blank your mind, and wait for the first thought to appear. This time, think of that thought, and think of everything else that's not that thought. So if the thought is "freedom," think of everything else that's anything but freedom.

In this exercise, you thought of one specific thing (the thought that entered your head) and everything else. You split the whole of creation into two parts. In a sense, this is the Source entering Wisdom.

Archetypes represent the purest form of something. We are mainly concerned with archetypal memories and archetypal people. You can think of archetypes as being people like Mozart in the field of composing, Elizabeth I of England in the field of courage and leadership, Shakespeare in the field of writing, Mother Teresa in the field of compassion, or Steve Jobs in the field of creativity. These are people who seem as if they are filled with a pure source of energy. The pathway that runs from the Source to Archetypes provides that source of energy. Somehow, these archetypal individuals have tapped into that pathway. In one way, they are blessed in being able to express this pure energy in the world. In other ways, they become trapped by their own uniqueness. Genius is often driven.

Exercise

Choose somebody you know, or know of, who is an archetype in this way. Consider how that person has taken the energy of the universe and manifested it in his or her own unique way. What is this way? What is that person's unique characteristic that makes him or her an archetype? Perhaps you chose Thomas Edison and invention. Perhaps you chose Rosa Parks and moral courage. Perhaps you chose Mozart and musical composition.

Imagine seeing that person in front of you. Step into that person and check in with your feelings. How does it feel to be manifesting the energy of the universe in that unique way?

There's a direct pathway from the Source to your True Unconscious (in some schools of Kabbalah, there is actually a hidden point between Tiferet, the True Unconscious, and Kether, the Source, called Da'ath, but I won't be discussing this point here). This means that your True Unconscious has the ability to tap into the Source—to tap into the mind of God, if you will. This is the pathway that mystics seek to open up through meditation or prayer. When this pathway opens, the mystic reaches a state of enlightenment that allows the Source to act directly through him or her.

Conclusion

We have come to the end of our discussion of the Tree of Life and Tree of Life Coaching. But as I hope I have shown you, within the Tree of Life, each ending is really nothing more than a new beginning.

You now have all the tools you need to understand and transform the lives of your clients. And you have all the tools you need to understand and transform your own life.

As you read these words, you're in a certain place, and you're at a certain time. But that context, that time and place, are the result of the energy that has flowed down your Tree of Life from the Source since the birth of time, down through each and every branch to where you are, here and now.

In the biggest picture of all, the Source represents the Big Bang, the birth of the universe itself, the breath of God entering reality. Yet your experience, your life, is the result of countless Trees of Life, of galaxies and stars, and of your ancestors. You, too, have many Trees of Life. You have a Tree of Life for your career. You have a Tree of Life for your relationships. You have a Tree of Life for your finances. You have a Tree of Life for your hobbies and pastimes. You have a Tree of Life for your entire life, and you have a Tree of Life for each year, each day, each moment. There are trees within trees, resulting in the amazing phenomenon known as YOU.

By studying the Tree of Life, you can become the arborist of your own life. You can plant acorns, nurture saplings, and grow mighty oak trees, or you can train tiny bonsai trees to fill each moment with joy.

And you can start now. The next time you're in a conversation with someone, begin to ask that person about his or her own Tree of Life. Remember to root it in a specific context, a specific time and place...

"When was the last time you did that? Where are you? What do you see?..."

And when that tree is firmly rooted, gently lead that person to explore the branches.

"What do you think about that? How are you seeing it?... How are you feeling?... Why are you doing that? What's important to you about that?... How did you learn that? When was the first time?... What else have you not been noticing about that, but when you do, everything will be different?"

And of course, ask yourself the same questions. And just because you found the answers, never stop asking. Something better—a new Tree of Life—is waiting to be born!

Appendix: Demonstration

The following example of Tree of Life Coaching was taken from a session with a client, John (not his real name). John has a difficult relationship with his father, who is separated from his mother. John has a great relationship with his mother. John is in his mid-twenties.

Coach: What do you want to work through today, John? [The opening]

Client: I want to change how I respond to somebody. I want to change how I respond to my father.

Coach: Can you tell me about a specific instance when you responded in a way you don't want to?

[As always, we want to ground the Tree of Life in a specific Real World context.]

Client: Yes, he called me on Wednesday night. I saw his number appear on my phone, and the only reason I answered it was because I didn't want him to leave me a voicemail that I would have to listen to later.

[You can begin to hear John provide elements of his Tree of Life, in this case including Rules: "I have to listen to voicemails that are left on my phone" and his Sensory Model of the World: "Not answering the phone now causes me to have an issue in the future."]

Coach: So you wanted to get it over with?

Client: Yes, though I really don't want to speak to him. So I answered the phone and he's miserable, and he immediately starts to lay into me for not calling him. Then he starts to give me attitude and tells me all the things I have to do. He tells me I have to come around and help him to move, and I have to do it on a certain day no matter what my schedule is, and I have to come to see him at the holidays...

[John tenses up his body and his face... He is showing a synesthesia. This lets the coach know that they have indeed found an appropriate context and that the Tree of Life that John is experiencing is the Tree of Life that is giving him the problem. The synesthesia is in the Emotion branch of the Tree of Life associated with this negative Tree of Life.]

Coach: What is that? [Coach replays the facial expression to John so they can further explore the problem Tree of Life.]

Client: It's like "no"... [This "no" is a word, so it's in the branch of Thought. The coach wants a little more information...]

Coach: It looks like it's more than just no... Isn't it?

Client: Yes, his energy is too much...

[John is defining the problem by the *quantity* of energy—"too much"—rather than the quality of the energy. In fact, the quality of the energy is much more likely to be the issue, and the coach challenges...]

Coach: Is it the energy…? How would it be if he called you up and was very excited: "John, you have to come and see this—it's absolutely amazing…"?

Client: That would be different. But there is a nastiness to the energy.

Coach: Tell me again why you don't want to pick up the phone?

[The coach asked this question because he wants to understand John's Sensory Model of the World. Simply speaking to a nasty person on the phone is not, by itself, sufficient to cause the problem that John is experiencing.]

Client: Because I know that when I speak to him, I will feel pressured to come and see him…

[Here John reveals a part of his Sensory Model of the World: speaking to his father *causes* him to feel pressured.]

Client: He never offers to come and pick me up, and it takes me hours to get to his house. [John doesn't drive a car for medical reasons and relies on public transportation.] He wants me to come around and help him, but he won't give me a ride. Everything has to be on his schedule.

[Here we have a more complete description of John's Sensory Model of the World: speaking to his father causes him to feel pressured, feeling pressured causes him to agree to visit his father, visiting his father causes him significant inconvenience, and this inconvenience outweighs what John sees as his father's contribution to the relationship.]

Coach: Why does he think you "have to"?

[Interestingly, John also begins to describe his father's Tree of Life. As you can begin to see, it is the clash between John's Tree of Life and his father's Tree of Life that is causing the difficulty. At some level, all interpersonal problems are caused by the clash between the Tree of Life of each of the individuals.]

Client: When we were growing up, he was never there for us, but he seems to think that because we are his children, we are his servants. And if we refuse, he gets nasty. I can't say no because there'll be all sorts of nastiness.

Coach: Are you making a picture inside your head? I see you looking over here.

[The coach explores the branch of Thought...]

Client: Yes, I'm seeing scenes from my childhood. There are a number of them—times when he was supposed to be there but wasn't because he was off getting drunk.

Coach: So when you picked up your phone and you saw it was him, how did you feel?

[This question completes the coach's exploration of the lower triad of John's Tree of Life...]

Client: [sighs and drops his head]

Coach: Where do you feel that?

Client: It's in my chest and stomach...

Coach: It looks heavy, like a weight.

Client: Yes, that's what it feels like, just like a weight.

[Coach shifts his physiology, and John follows.]

Coach: That's how you been. How do you want to be different?

Client: I want to be able to cut him off. Not totally, but I want to be able to say, "No, I can't do that."

Coach: So that's what you'd be doing. How would you be feeling?

[The coach invites John to identify a new emotion that might go along with the new behavior, but as we shall see, John has difficulty finding a suitable emotion...]

Client: I want to say confidence, but it's not confidence—it's something else...

Coach: So aside from that weight you have been feeling, what's everything else you could be seeing, that would throw more light on the situation?

[The coach uses inductive language to lead John into Wisdom. You will notice that the coach changes the sensory system from feeling, "weight," to seeing and uses "light" as the opposite of weight. As we shall see, the question doesn't work perfectly!]

Client: [John's eyes drift upward and from side to side for a few moments.] I'm not sure...

[Being "not sure" indicates that John visited Wisdom but did not find a good landing place. The coach now asks John where he would like to land!]

Coach: You're not sure. And when you're not sure, how you want to feel instead?

Client: I just want the answer, that's all! I want to feel different, but I want the answer...

["Answer" indicates that John may have landed somewhere in the left-hand column—"the answer" could be in the branch of Thought or the branch of Rules. Because John ended in the left column, the coach decides to move up to the branch of Archetypes in search of this missing answer...]

Coach: Who do you want the answer from? From me?... From yourself?... From your father?... [John shrugs.] If you could be anyone who already has the answer, who would that be?

Client: I would like to be somebody who owns the space, who doesn't get pushed around...

Coach: And who would that be?

Client: I'm not sure...

[John is remaining stuck in the Tree of Life of the problem. The coach decides to use and even exaggerate this problem Tree of Life...]

Coach: Well you know people who don't own the space, people who do get pushed around, right?

Client: Yes.

Coach: People who get pushed around and come back for more...

Client: Yes!

[.. And now switch that to the opposite...]

Coach: So who is the opposite of that?

Client: I have a good friend who's like that. He owns his space, and nobody pushes *him* around.

Coach: Great! Now what is the distinction that he makes—is it him [John nods] who lets him own the space that makes it impossible for him to be pushed around?

[The coach is leading John back up to Wisdom in this new archetype's Tree of Life. It will take a couple of attempts…]

Client: He would say something like, "If you want to be that way, that's fine, but it's on you." [John describes the archetype's behavior.]

Coach: And what distinction is he drawing that makes him do that—how does he know that's the thing to do?

Client: It's a lack of respect, it's an insult, and it's over.

[John straightens and his physiology shifts into something more "forceful."]

Coach: So it's an insult. How do you know if you are being insulted?

[The coach switches to using the pronoun *you* instead of *he*.]

Client: It's a feeling…

[John is clearly beginning to feel more resourceful at this stage based on his physiology…]

Coach: And where is that feeling?

Client: It's strange—it's not an emotion, it's a feeling outside of me like this... [John crosses his hands and scissors them open.] It's like I'm cutting...

[John is, as usual, quite left-brained and tries to shift into the left-hand column and the branch of Thought. The coach wants to keep him in the branch of Emotion, at least until the feeling is located in the body.]

Coach: And what happens when there's that [coach copies the gesture]... cutting?

Client: It takes all my stuff away—all my thoughts and feelings—and moves them away... [John gestures to his left. He is "normally organized," and this represents his "past" in the NLP timeline model.]

[John is essentially allowing the old Tree of Life to move away. However, he is not yet stepping into a new Tree of Life, as we shall see shortly.]

Coach: And then what happens?

Client: If they do it again, I don't care anymore.

[John is telling us what he *doesn't* feel.]

Coach: And when there's that [coach repeats gesture] and it takes all your stuff away [coach gestures to the client's left], what are you thinking?

Client: All those old thoughts have left—they're over there. I'm not thinking them anymore...

[John is telling us what he is not thinking. It's time to begin to build a new Tree of Life.]

Coach: That's great, and what are you thinking instead?

Client: I'm thinking, "That's their stuff, not mine." [Again, John comes up with a negative.]

Coach: How do you know that—how do you know that's their stuff and not yours? What are you seeing that lets you know that's their stuff and not yours?

Client: I see their pattern.

Coach: So you see them doing their pattern, and that gives you the power?

Client: Yes.

[The coach decides that it's time to shift back to the branch of Emotion…]

Coach: And when you're seeing their pattern, and you have the power, how are you feeling?

Client: I feel free, but I also feel sad.

Coach: Where do you feel free, in your body?

Client: In my shoulders. I guess I feel the sadness in my heart because things could have been different but weren't different.

[John's sadness arises from a value that is missing in the relationship—we will come back to that shortly. In the meantime, the coach focuses on the positive feeling "freedom" and seeks to spread it through the rest of the new, resourceful Tree of Life.]

Coach: And as you are feeling free and you see the number appear on your phone, what does that cause you to do?

[With the last question, the coach was seeking to take the new, resourceful feeling—"freedom"—and the new, resourceful thought of seeing the other person's pattern, and to spread these down into John's Sensory Model of the World by asking what the phone call would cause him to do.]

Client: [Sighs] There is still something there...

Coach: I see that!

Client: There is a fear there...

Coach: A fear of what?... a fear that you'll fall back into the old pattern, or a fear of the argument?

Client: Yes, that I'll fall back because if I do that, if I cut him off like that, it will start a fight, and I'll be the one who caves. I don't know what else to do.

[This is a fear of the unknown because John is now in an unknown and untested Tree of Life. The coach has to help John explore how this new Tree of Life is going to help him. This is called a "future-pace" in NLP.]

Coach: Well, that's because we haven't explored what you can do instead—we haven't gotten there yet! Be patient!

Client: OK! [Laughs]

Coach: Going back to your friend—the one who owns the space—does he start fights?

Client: No, but it's different because of my father. I know his pattern. [Notice that John is remaining within the new Tree of Life by saying he knows his father's pattern.] I know how he is going to respond. He's going to start a fight, and then I will have to give in.

Coach: Does he physically attack you? [Ecology check, and to make sure John understands that the "fight" he describes is only verbal.]

Client: No.

Coach: So he attacks you verbally?

Client: Yes.

Coach: So he attacks you either way...

Client: What...?

Coach: You said that whenever he calls you up, he starts the conversation by attacking you... So he is attacking you either way, no matter what you do, is he not?

[This is a reframe of John's current Sensory Model of the World, which is "If I fail to give him what he wants, my father will verbally attack me." This is reframed to "My father will attack me either way."]

Client: Yes, I guess that's right.

[As the coach, you always want your clients to commit to whatever changes they have made so far. Guessing isn't good enough!]

Coach: You guess it's right, or you know it's right?

Client: It's right. He attacks me either way. The difference is the level of intensity. If I cut him off like that, he will escalate and start saying all sorts of nasty things about me.

Coach: This may sound like a strange question, but I really want to know. Do the things he says bother you because he says them or because you think they're true?

[The coaches seeking to identify any adverse archetypal memories that John's father may be triggering, which would require a reimprinting.]

Client: They're not true. I know that they are not true. [John is very congruent when he says this.] But he shouldn't say them to me—he's my father.

Coach: No one should say those things to you. [The coach wants to make sure that this new Tree of Life is generalized and doesn't just apply within the context of John's father.] But you're right—especially not your father. He does this with everyone? So you're seeing his pattern.

Client: I just wish it were different. [Once more, John brings up the "hidden" value that is underlying his sadness and this wish that things were different. The coach is now going to use this value to accelerate the changes that are already taking place.]

Coach: Have you heard the saying, "If you always do what you've always done, you'll always get what you always got"?

Client: Yes, of course—you're always saying that!

Coach: It's true—you saw my pattern! And he's been running his pattern, right? You see that, do you not?

Client: Yes.

Coach: And I see that you've been running your pattern—giving in. And nothing has been changing. Do you think it's time to try something different?

Client: [Laughs] Yes!

[Now we are going to run the new Tree of Life and find out what happens.]

Coach: So what happens if you try something different?

Client: He's going to escalate.

Coach: Right, like climbing a mountain. [The coach introduces a new archetypal metaphor—one that he has used before with John that represents a difficult but rewarding struggle.] And then what happens to him?

Client: I'll hang up.

[The coach wants John to consider how his father might respond to this new Tree of Life so the scenario can be played out in John's imagination. Instead, John describes his own responses. We have to push further.]

Coach: Maybe, but if you don't hang up, what happens to *him*? What happens to him at the top of the mountain?

Client: I'll feel bad…

[John sticks with the implications for himself—for John…]

Coach: Maybe, but what I'm asking you is this: if you stay on the phone and you don't give in, what happens to him?

Client: I don't know.

Coach: I know you don't know, because you've never tried it! Play it out in your mind now. What happens when he gets to the top of his mountain?

Client: He slams the phone down!

Coach: OK, great—maybe he does. That would be something different. And then what happens the next time he calls you and you don't give in?

Client: Maybe he slams the phone down again.

Coach: Maybe he does, he calls you a second time, yells at you, and slams the phone down. What happens the third time, the fourth time, the fifth time?? He's got to go over the peak and to the far side of the mountain. You don't know what's there because you've never tried it. [John is smiling.] That's right—play that out in your mind. What happens when he gets to the top of his mountain?

[John begins laughing.]

That's right. And it's not enough for you to let him go to the top of the mountain—you have to encourage him, you have to lead him up there, because until he gets there, neither of you know what's on the other side. To give your father the opportunity to change—for things to be different between you—you have to take him to the top of the mountain and see what's on the other side.

Client: I'm not sure what's on the other side of the mountain …

Coach: That's right. And you won't know till you get there. But I guarantee you that when you take him to the top of the mountain in your next phone call, he's never going to be the same again. He may not enjoy the experience, but he's not going to repeat it.

[The coach is now exaggerating the process of "not giving in"—making it active and giving control back to John.]

Client: I like that!

Coach: It's not going to be enough for you to just not give in. You have to be prepared to take him to the top of the mountain, all the way up. You've got to be prepared to allow him to escalate until there is nothing more left for him to do. And you've got to be ready to have fun with it.

Client: I think in the past, I was afraid to do that because I was afraid I would lose out on something. But he doesn't do anything for me. So what have I got to lose?

Coach: He could cut your allowance…

[John is now arguing in support of his own change. The coach changes tack and begins to argue against the change, but in a ridiculous way…]

Client: [Laughing] He doesn't even buy me a birthday present!

[The coach now installs the work just done in the branch of Thought…]

Coach: And when you're not thinking of this old stuff that's in your past now [gestures to John's left], you can be thinking about how high he has gone on the mountain, and how far he might have to go, and what might be on the other side for both of you…

And the next time he calls—not the next time, but the time after, when you've already seen him go to the top of the

263

mountain—you can just say, "Let's save us both some time. I know you think I'm X, Y, Z, but what else have you called to say?"

[And now the coach moves to the branch of Energy, meaning values, by leveraging the hidden value and end state energy.]

Now, it may be entertaining to take him to the top of the mountain and let him see that there's nothing of value there for him. But what's really important is that you're giving him the opportunity to go over to the other side—to change. And he will change, even though you can't know exactly what that change will be.

Client: It's fun!

Coach: Right! It's like a game. What is that energy like for you?

Client: It's Dude-ness [reference to *The Big Lebowski*, one of John's favorite films].

Coach: Right! It's taking that negative energy from outside and converting it into a transformative experience.

Client: It holds the room together!

Coach: So he calls up, and you see his number…

Client: [Laughs] Dude-ness! It holds the room together!

Coach: You go around to his house and it's 9 o'clock in the morning, he's on his fifth beer, and he wants to pick a fight.

Client: [Laughing] It's ridiculous!

[This is followed by more generalization, future pacing, and testing to make sure the new Tree of Life is firmly rooted.]

Other Books By This Publisher

Deep Trance Identification: Unconscious Modeling and Mastery for Coaches,
Hypnosis Practitioners, and Everyday People
By Shawn Carson and Jess Marion with John Overdurf

Keeping the Brain in Mind: Practical Neuroscience for Coaches, Therapists, and
Hypnosis Practitioners
By Shawn Carson and Melissa Tiers

Quit: The Hypnotists Handbook to Running Effective Stop Smoking Sessions
By Jess Marion, Sarah Carson, and Shawn Carson

The Swish (NLP Mastery Series)
By Shawn Carson and Jess Marion

The Visual Squash (NLP Mastery Series)
By Jess Marion and Shawn Carson

The Meta Pattern (NLP Mastery Series)
By Sarah Carson and Shawn Carson

The BEAT Pattern (NLP Mastery Series)
By Sarah Carson and Shawn Carson

I Quit
By Jess Marion, Sarah Carson and Shawn Carson

Printed in Great Britain
by Amazon

24730178R00149